MAP COLLECTIONS
IN THE
UNITED STATES AND CANADA

A Directory
Second Edition

MAP COLLECTIONS
IN THE
UNITED STATES AND CANADA

MAP COLLECTIONS
IN THE
UNITED STATES AND CANADA

A Directory
Second Edition

compiled by the
Directory Revision Committee
David K. Carrington
Chairman

A Project of the Geography and Map Division

SPECIAL LIBRARIES ASSOCIATION

New York

1970

Standard Book Number 87111-190-X
Library of Congress Catalog Card Number 72-101336
© 1970 by Special Libraries Association
235 Park Avenue South, New York 10003

Printed in the United States of America

CONTENTS

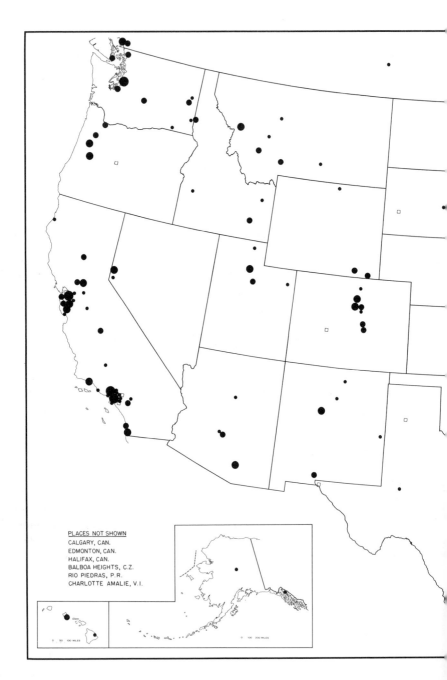

PLACES NOT SHOWN
CALGARY, CAN.
EDMONTON, CAN.
HALIFAX, CAN.
BALBOA HEIGHTS, C.Z.
RIO PIEDRAS, P.R.
CHARLOTTE AMALIE, V.I.

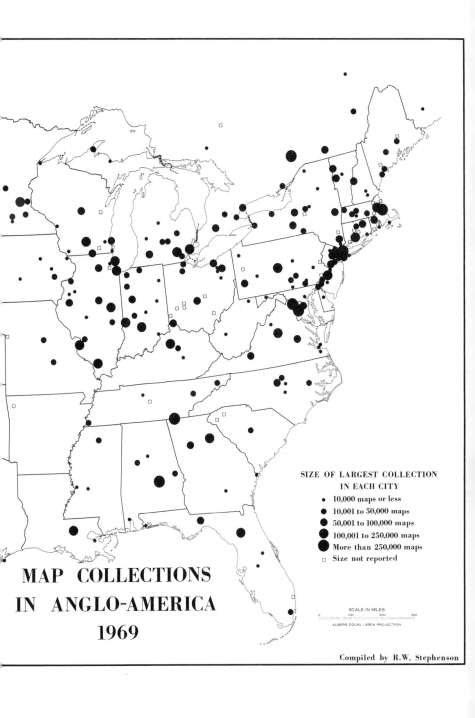

SIZE OF LARGEST COLLECTION
IN EACH CITY
- • 10,000 maps or less
- ● 10,001 to 50,000 maps
- ● 50,001 to 100,000 maps
- ● 100,001 to 250,000 maps
- ● More than 250,000 maps
- ▫ Size not reported

MAP COLLECTIONS
IN ANGLO-AMERICA
1969

SCALE IN MILES
0   100   200   300
ALBERS EQUAL - AREA PROJECTION

Compiled by R.W. Stephenson

PREFACE

Sixteen years ago the Geography and Map Division of Special Libraries Association published *Map Collections in the United States and Canada*. The directory, which was compiled under the direction of Mrs. Marie C. Goodman, has been an invaluable reference for information about cartographic collections in Anglo-America. The passage of time, however, has left its mark on this fine publication.

In 1968, therefore, SLA's Geography and Map Division designated a committee to compile an up-to-date directory. A mailing list of some 1,300 university, special, and public libraries was prepared from many sources including the 1954 *Directory of Map Collections in the United States and Canada*, the *American Library Directory*, Schwendeman's *Directory of College Geography of the United States*, Kruzas' *Directory of Special Libraries and Information Centers*, and the map depository lists of the Army Topographic Command (formerly the Army Map Service) and the United States Geological Survey. In addition, special regional lists were supplied by Mary Galneder, University of Wisconsin-Madison, Kathleen Brennan, Western Washington State College (Bellingham) and Mary Schell, California State Library (Sacramento).

Questionnaires, with explanatory letters, were mailed October 1, 1968. Follow-up letters, accompanied by questionnaires, were mailed on November 15 and December 1, 1968. The combined mailings resulted in a 73 percent response —a total of 958 returns. From these, 605 collections were selected for inclusion in the revised directory. Excluding 22 private collectors reported in the 1954 directory, this represents a 20 percent increase in the number of citations in the present list. Because of the difficulty in identifying private collections and in determining their relative accessibility to the public, the Directory Revision Committee decided to omit such collections in the new edition.

Entries are arranged alphabetically by city, within a state or province. The entry number appears in boldface and the library name appears in capital letters, followed by street address and/or box number, ZIP code or postal zone in parentheses, and telephone number, with area code and extension. The name of the map librarian, or person responsible for the administration of the map collection, with his or her official title, completes the address statement. Descriptive information for each collection includes size of staff, collection size, annual accessions, area and subject specializations, special cartographic collections, depository agreements, service restrictions, interlibrary loan policy, reproduction facilities, map library publications, and in some instances, an occasional explanatory note. Collections for which data were obtained from sources other than the questionnaire are noted with either an asterisk (*) or a brief statement.

The index is arranged alphabetically, with numbers referring to individual entries rather than pages. Much of the information found in the collection descriptions has been indexed with the exception of a few repetitious subject terms and area names, such as "geography," "topography," "history," "geology," "United States," etc.

The chairman of the Directory Revision Committee is indebted to the many individuals who assisted in the compilation of this directory. Muriel H. Parry and Paula M. Strain, both past Chairmen of SLA's Geography and Map Division provided counsel and guidance during the preliminary planning and development stages of the project. Stanley Stevens and Dr. Walter W. Ristow assisted with the planning and compilation of the questionnaire and cover letter. A debt of gratitude is owed the Directory Revision Committee members themselves for the many, many hours of hard work. Mrs. Sylvia L. Alexander, Muriel Parry, Andrew M. Modelski, Richard W. Stephenson, and John A. Wolter performed most of the editorial tasks. In addition, Mr. Modelski supervised the typing of the manuscript. Mr. Stephenson, who served in many ways as associate editor during the project, is due special recognition for developing the index and designing the map which accompanies this edition.

David K. Carrington, Chairman
Directory Revision Committee
Geography and Map Division, SLA

November 1969

ABBREVIATIONS

ACIC	Aeronautical Chart and Information Center
BRGM	Bureau de Recherches Géologiques et Minières
DOS	Directorate of Overseas Surveys
ESSA	Environmental Science Services Administration
ext.	extension
geol	geologic
GSC	Geological Survey of Canada
IMW	International Map of the World
Libn.	Librarian
NOC	Naval Oceanographic Charts
NTS	National Topographic System (Canada)
o.p.	out of print
P.O.	Post Office
Tel.	Telephone
topo	topographic
TOPOCOM	United States Army Topographic Command (formerly the United States Army Map Service)
USAF	United States Air Force
USC&GS	United States Coast and Geodetic Survey
USDA	United States Department of Agriculture
USGS	United States Geological Survey
USSR	Union of Soviet Socialist Republics
v.	volume(s)
*	data obtained from sources other than the Map Directory Questionnaire

ALABAMA

Auburn

1 AUBURN UNIVERSITY, LIBRARY. (36830) Tel. 205/826-4500. Miss Mary E. Wilbanks, Special Collections Libn.
Staff: 2 full time; 2 part time.
Size: 40,000 maps; 8,600 aerial photographs.
Annual accessions: several hundred maps.
Area specialization: Alabama.
Subject specialization: topography.
Depository for: TOPOCOM; USGS (topo, geol).
Serves: University; public.
Interlibrary loan: not available.
Reproduction facilities: photocopy; Xerox.

Birmingham

2 BIRMINGHAM PUBLIC LIBRARY, THE RUCKER AGEE COLLECTION. (35203) Tel. 205/252-5106. George Stewart.
Staff: 2 part time.
Size: 2,025 maps; 598 atlases; 6 globes; 6 relief models; 71 gazetteers.
Annual accessions: 100 maps; 150 atlases.
Area specializations: southeastern United States; Alabama.
Subject specializations: historical cartography; discovery and exploration; Civil War.
Special cartographic collection: Agee Collection—historical and regional maps from the Age of Discovery to the present.
Serves: public (by permission).
Interlibrary loan: not available.
Reproduction facility: Xerox.
Publications: The Rucker Agee Collection of the Birmingham Public Library (1964).
Note: The Collection contains some 1,500 volumes of related material, books on celestial naviagation and pilotage, engineering, geography, economics, and history as well as bibliographies and printed catalogs of outstanding map and atlas collections.

3 SAMFORD UNIVERSITY, LIBRARY, SPECIAL COLLECTIONS, 800 Lakeshore Drive. (35209) Tel. 205/870-2846. Mrs. Fanna K. Bee, Libn.
Staff: 1 part time.
Size: 896 maps; 71 atlases.
Area specializations: southern United States; Alabama; Indian territories.
Subject specialization: history.
Serves: University; public.
Interlibrary loan: not available.
Reproduction facilities: photocopy; Xerox; microfilm.

Maxwell Air Force Base

4 AIR UNIVERSITY, LIBRARY, CARTOGRAPHY DIVISION. (36112) Tel. 205/265-5521, ext. 2313. John D. Ashmore, Chief.
Staff: 5 full time.

Size: 400,000 maps; 20 atlases; 6 globes; 700 relief models; 13,000 aerial
photographs; 200 gazetteers.
Annual accessions: 10,000 maps; 100 relief models; 1,000 aerial photographs.
Area specialization: worldwide.
Subject specialization: comprehensive.
Serves: University.
Interlibrary loan: not available.
Reproduction facility: Xerox.

Mobile

5 MOBILE PUBLIC LIBRARY, SPECIAL COLLECTIONS DIVISION, 701
Government Street. (36602) Tel. 205/433-0484, ext. 27. Mrs. Ruth Warren,
Head.
Staff: 2 full time; 2 part time.
Size: 150 maps; 4 atlases.
Area specialization: Mobile county and city.
Subject specialization: history.
Special cartographic collections: Louis Troost maps of Mobile, 1840 (7 volumes of
drawings, on microfilm); Official Maps—War of the Rebellion.
Serves: public.
Interlibrary loan: not available.
Reproduction facilities: Xerox; microfilm.

University

6 UNIVERSITY OF ALABAMA, DEPARTMENT OF GEOLOGY—GE-
OGRAPHY. P. O. Box 1945. (35486) Tel. 205/348-5095. Eugene M. Wilson,
Assistant Professor.
Size: 30,000 maps; 5 globes; 12 relief models; aerial photographs of Alabama.
Depository for: TOPOCOM.
Serves: University.
Interlibrary loan: not available.

7 UNIVERSITY OF ALABAMA, MAIN LIBRARY, ALABAMA COLLEC-
TION. (35486) Tel. 205/348-6234. Mrs. Jeanette Newsome, Special Collec-
tions Libn.
Size: 1,508 maps; 33 atlases; 3 gazetteers.
Annual accessions: 20 maps.
Area specialization: Alabama.
Serves: University; public (courtesy card holders only).
Interlibrary loan: not available.
Reproduction facility: Xerox.

ALASKA

Auke Bay

8 U. S. FISH AND WILDLIFE SERVICE, BUREAU OF COMMERCIAL
FISHERIES, FISHERIES RESEARCH LIBRARY, Box 155. (99821) Tel.
907/789-7231, ext. 125. Elmer Landingham.
Staff: 1 part time.
Size: 2,900 maps; 26 atlases; 1 globe; 1 relief model; 48 aerial photographs; 24
gazetteers.

Annual accessions: 250 maps.
Area specialization: Alaska..
Subject specialization: geography.
Depository for: USGS (topo, geol—Alaska).
Serves: employees.
Interlibrary loan: available.
Reproduction facilities: Xerox; microfilm.

College

9 ALASKA (STATE) DIVISION OF MINES AND GEOLOGY, P. O. Box 5-300. (99701) Tel. 907/479-2202, ext. 25. Mary E. Shrewsbury, Mining Information Specialist.
Staff: 1 full time.
Size: 2,100 maps; 805 aerial photographs.
Area specialization: Alaska.
Subject specializations: geology; geochemistry.
Serves: public.
Interlibrary loan: not available.
Reproduction facility: Xerox.

10 UNIVERSITY OF ALASKA, LIBRARY. (99701) Tel. 907/479-7224.
Size: not reported. Library receives maps through selective depository program.
Serves: University; public.
Interlibrary loan: not available.
Reproduction facilities: Xerox; microfilm.

ARIZONA

Flagstaff

11 MUSEUM OF NORTHERN ARIZONA, LIBRARY, MAP COLLECTION, P. O. Box 1389. (86001) Tel. 602/774-2433, ext. 25. Katharine Bartlett, Libn.
Staff: 1 part time.
Size: 3,534 maps; 10 atlases; 1 relief model; 3,293 aerial photographs.
Annual accessions: 145 maps; 30 aerial photographs.
Area specializations: southwestern United States; Colorado Plateau.
Subject specializations: topography; archaeology; geology; Indians.
Serves: public.
Interlibrary loan: not available.
Reproduction facility: Xerox.

12 NORTHERN ARIZONA UNIVERSITY, LIBRARY. (86001) Tel. 602/523-3791.
Size: 2,275 maps; 15 atlases; 1 globe; 10 gazetteers.
Area specialization: northern Arizona.
Subject specialization: topography.
Depository for: USGS (topo).
Serves: University; public.
Interlibrary loan: not available.
Reproduction facility: photocopy.

Phoenix

13 ARIZONA (STATE) DEPARTMENT OF LIBRARY AND ARCHIVES, 3rd Floor Capitol. (85007) Tel. 602/271-5101. Mrs. Marguerite B. Cooley, Director.

Size: 6,000 maps.
Area specializations: southwestern United States; Arizona.
Depository for: USGS (topo, geol); Arizona State.
Serves: public.
Interlibrary loan: not available.
Reproduction facilities: photocopy; microfilm.

14 ARIZONA (STATE) DEPARTMENT OF MINERAL RESOURCES, Mineral Building, Fairgrounds. (85007) Tel. 602/258-6681. Frank P. Knight, Director.

Size: 2,000 maps; 11 atlases.
Area specialization: Arizona.
Subject specializations: mines and mining.
Special cartographic collections: mine and claim maps and sketches.
Depository for: California and New Mexico state maps.
Serves: public.
Interlibrary loan: not available.

15 PHOENIX PUBLIC LIBRARY, REFERENCE DIVISION, MAPS SECTION, 12 East McDowell Road. (85004) Tel. 602/262-6557. Miss Susan Quinlivan, Libn.

Staff: 1 part time.
Size: 1,280 maps; 217 atlases; 8 globes; 10 gazetteers.
Annual accessions: 1,000 maps; 40 atlases.
Area specializations: Arizona; southwestern United States.
Subject specializations: history; topography; geology.
Serves: public.
Interlibrary loan: not available.
Reproduction facility: photocopy.

Tempe

16 ARIZONA STATE UNIVERSITY, LIBRARY, MAP COLLECTION. (85281) Tel. 602/961-3451. Roland McKay.

Size: 11,000 maps; 1 relief model; 25 gazetteers.
Annual accessions: 1,000 maps.
Area specializations: Western Hemisphere; Africa.
Subject specialization: geography.
Special cartographic collections: Hulbert's *Crown Collection of Photographs of American Maps*; plans of cities of London, Westminster, and Southwark.
Depository for: TOPOCOM; USGS (topo, geol).
Serves: University; public.
Interlibrary loan: not available.
Reproduction facility: Xerox.

Tucson

17 ARIZONA (STATE) BUREAU OF MINES, University of Arizona. (85721) Tel. 602/884-2733. Dr. Richard T. Moore, Geologist.

Staff: 1 part time.
Size: 1,500 maps; 5 atlases; 700 aerial photographs.

Annual accessions: 30 maps; 5 atlases.
Area specialization: Arizona.
Subject specializations: geology; topography.
Depository for: USGS (topo, geol).
Serves: public.
Interlibrary loan: not available.
Reproduction facility: photocopy.

18 TUCSON PUBLIC LIBRARY, 200 South Sixth Avenue. (85701) Tel. 602/ 791-4393. Mrs. Lynne M. Phillips, Head, Reference Section.
Size: small reference collection.
Area specializations: Arizona; Tucson.
Special cartographic collection: Ferguson map of city of Tucson (1862).
Serves: public.
Interlibrary loan: not available.
Reproduction facility: photocopy.

19 UNIVERSITY OF ARIZONA, LIBRARY, MAP COLLECTION. (85721) Tel. 602/884-2596. Miss Mary Blakeley, Map Libn.
Staff: 3 full time; 2 part time.
Size: 80,000 maps; 800 atlases; 7 globes; 45 relief models; 14,600 aerial photographs; 150 gazetteers.
Annual accessions: 5,000 maps; 150 atlases; 15 gazetteers.
Area specializations: southwestern United States; Arizona; Mexico.
Subject specializations: geology; topography; history.
Depository for: TOPOCOM; USGS (topo, geol).
Serves: University; public.
Interlibrary loan: available.
Reproduction facilities: photocopy; Xerox.
Publication: map library brochure.

ARKANSAS

Fayetteville

20 UNIVERSITY OF ARKANSAS, DEPARTMENT OF GEOLOGY. (72701) Tel. 501/575-3355. James H. Quinn, Department Chairman.
Subject specialization: topography.
Depository for: USGS (topo).
Serves: University; public.
Interlibrary loan: available.

21 UNIVERSITY OF ARKANSAS, GENERAL LIBRARY*. (72701) Tel. 501/575-4101.
Depository for: TOPOCOM.

CALIFORNIA

Arcata

22 HUMBOLDT STATE COLLEGE, LIBRARY. (95521) Tel. 707/826-3416. Eric Simms, Libn. General maps; Charles Bloom, Libn. Science maps.
Staff: 3 part time.
Size: 3,000 maps; 100 atlases; 3 globes; 50 relief models; 5 gazetteers.

Annual accessions: 250 maps; 5 atlases.
Area specializations: Humboldt county; northern California.
Subject specializations: local history; topography; natural resources; coastal maps.
Serves: College; public.
Interlibrary loan: available.
Reproduction facility: Xerox.

Bakersfield

23 KERN COUNTY LIBRARY, REFERENCE SERVICES, 1315 Truxtun Avenue. (93301) Tel. 805/327-2111, ext. 2635. Miss Mary Weeks, Geology-Mining—Petroleum Libn.
Staff: 1 part time.
Size: 3,846 maps; 24 wall maps; 30 atlases; 6 globes; 1 relief model; 115 gazetteers.
Annual accessions: 200 maps; 3 atlases; 5 gazetteers.
Area specializations: California; Arizona; Nevada.
Subject specializations: topography; geology.
Serves: public.
Interlibrary loan: not available.
Reproduction facilities: photocopy; Xerox; microfilm.

Berkeley

24 BERKELEY PUBLIC LIBRARY. (94701) Tel. 415/843-0800. Mrs. Evelyn Gahtan, Reference Libn.
Staff: 1 part time.
Size: 2,600 maps; 25 atlases; 1 globe; 3 gazetteers.
Serves: public.
Interlibrary loan: not available.
Reproduction facility: photocopy.

25 UNIVERSITY OF CALIFORNIA, BANCROFT LIBRARY. (94720) Tel. 415/642-3781. Robert H. Becker.
Staff: 1 part time.
Size: 12,803 maps; 2 atlases; 4 gazetteers.
Area specialization: western North America.
Subject specialization: history.
Serves: University; public.
Interlibrary loan: not available.
Reproduction facilities: photocopy; microfilm.
Publication: Catalog of Printed Maps in the Bancroft Library.

26 UNIVERSITY OF CALIFORNIA, EARTH SCIENCES LIBRARY. (94720) Tel. 415/642-2997. Mrs. Beatrice Lukens, Libn.
Staff: 1 part time.
Size: 21,110 maps; 51 atlases; 1 globe.
Annual accessions: 2,000 maps.
Area specializations: western United States; Alaska; Hawaii.
Subject specializations: topography; geology.
Depository for: USGS (topo, geol).
Serves: University; public.
Interlibrary loan: not available.
Reproduction facilities: photocopy; Xerox; microfilm.

27   UNIVERSITY OF CALIFORNIA, EAST ASIATIC LIBRARY. (94720) Tel. 415/642-2556. Charles E. Hamilton, Acting Head.

Size: 12,500 maps.

Area specializations: Far East; Japan; Korea; China; Mongolia; Tibet.

Special cartographic collections: Japanese folded maps, chiefly wood-block, copperplate and manuscript from 17th to early 20th century.

Interlibrary loan: not available.

Reproduction facilities: photocopy; Xerox; microfilm.

28   UNIVERSITY OF CALIFORNIA, GEOGRAPHY DEPARTMENT, MAP LIBRARY, Room 515, Earth Sciences Building. (94720) Tel. 415/642-3903. Phillip Wallick.

Staff: 1 full time.

Size: 30,000 maps; 65 atlases; 10 globes; 10 relief models; 3,000 aerial photographs; 2 gazetteers.

Annual accessions: 500 maps; 5 atlases; 250 aerial photographs.

Area specializations: western United States; California; Central and South America.

Subject specializations: cultural, physical, and regional geography.

Serves: University.

Interlibrary loan: available (restricted).

Reproduction facility: Xerox.

29   UNIVERSITY OF CALIFORNIA, GENERAL LIBRARY, MAP ROOM. (94720) Tel. 415/642-4940. Miss Sheila Dowd, Map Libn.

Staff: 3 part time.

Size: 117,000 maps; 92 atlases; 1 globe; 12 relief models; 3,664 aerial photographs; 140 gazetteers.

Annual accessions: 10,000 maps.

Subject specializations: political geography; topography.

Special cartographic collection: De Vries Collection of old maps, atlases, and geographical works is deposited with the Library, and is housed in the Rare Books Collection.

Depository for: TOPOCOM; USGS (topo); USC&GS.

Serves: University; public.

Interlibrary loan: not available.

Reproduction facilities: photocopy; Xerox; microfilm.

30   UNIVERSITY OF CALIFORNIA, WATER RESOURCES CENTER ARCHIVES, Room 40, North Gate Hall. (94720) Tel. 415/642-2666. Gerald J. Giefer, Libn.

Staff: 3 full time; 3 part time.

Size: 300 maps.

Annual accessions: 20 maps.

Area specialization: California.

Subject specialization: water resources.

Serves: University; public.

Interlibrary loan: available.

Reproduction facilities: photocopy; Xerox.

Chico

31   CHICO STATE COLLEGE, DEPARTMENT OF GEOGRAPHY. (95926) Tel. 916/345-6478. Arthur E. Karinen, Department Head.

Size: 15,000 maps; 100 atlases; 3 globes; 500 aerial photographs.

Serves: College.
Interlibrary loan: not available.

32 CHICO STATE COLLEGE, LIBRARY, SCIENCE AND TECHNOLOGY DIVISION. (95926) Tel. 916/345-6479. J. Kent Stephens, Science and Technology Libn.
Staff: 2 part time.
Size: 8,872 maps; 10 atlases; 2 globes; 7 relief models.
Annual accessions: 2,500 maps; 10 atlases.
Area specializations: California; United States.
Subject specializations: topography; geology; local history.
Depository for: USGS (topo, geol); California State Division of Mines and Geology.
Serves: University; Public.
Interlibrary loan: not available.
Reproduction facility: Xerox.

Claremont

33 CLAREMONT COLLEGES, HANNOLD LIBRARY*, Ninth and Dartmouth Streets. (91711) Tel. 213/626-8511, ext. 2215. Robert F. Teare, Assistant Libn.
Depository for: TOPOCOM.

Davis

34 UNIVERSITY OF CALIFORNIA AT DAVIS, UNIVERSITY LIBRARY, MAP COLLECTION. (95616) Tel. 916/752-1624. Edward C. Jestes, Map Reference Libn.
Staff: 2 part time.
Size: 23,187 maps; 1,000 atlases; 20 relief models; 6 gazetteers.
Annual accessions: 5,372 maps.
Area specialization: western North America.
Subject specializations: soils; vegetation; climatology; land use.
Depository for: USGS (topo, geol—western United States).
Serves: University; public.
Interlibrary loan: available.
Reproduction facility: Xerox.

Fresno

35 FRESNO STATE COLLEGE, LIBRARY. (93726) Tel. 209/487-2174. A. Zane Clark, Senior Reference Libn.
Staff: 1 part time.
Size: 34,247 maps; 183 atlases; 6 globes; 147 gazetteers.
Annual accessions: 1,784 maps; 10 atlases.
Subject specializations: topography; geology.
Depository for: TOPOCOM; USGS (geol).
Serves: College; public.
Interlibrary loan: not available.
Reproduction facility: Xerox.

Fullerton

36 ORANGE COUNTY STATE COLLEGE, GEOGRAPHY DEPARTMENT, MAP LIBRARY*. (92634) Tel. 213/871-8000, ext. 46.
Depository for: TOPOCOM.

Glendale

37 GLENDALE PUBLIC LIBRARY, 319 East Harvard. (91205) Tel. 213/242-1157. Margaret V. Peterson, Documents Libn.
Staff: 2 part time.
Size: 2,400 maps; 91 atlases; 10 gazetteers.
Annual accessions: 120 maps; 2 atlases.
Area specializations: United States; California.
Subject specializations: topography; geology; history; Civil War; natural resources.
Serves: public.
Interlibrary loan: available.
Reproduction facility: Xerox.

Hayward

38 CALIFORNIA STATE COLLEGE AT HAYWARD, DEPARTMENT OF GEOGRAPHY-ANTHROPOLOGY, 25800 Hillary Street. (94542) Tel. 415/538-8000, ext. 221. R. E. Winter, Assistant Professor.
Staff: 1 part time.
Size: 10,000 maps; 200 atlases; 20 globes; 190 relief models; 7,000 aerial photographs.
Annual accessions: 3,000 maps.
Area specialization: Asia.
Subject specialization: topography.
Depository for: USGS (topo).
Serves: College; public.
Interlibrary loan: not available.
Reproduction facility: Xerox.

La Habra

39 CHEVRON OIL FIELD RESEARCH COMPANY, LIBRARY, P.O. Box 446. (90631) Tel. 213/691-2241, ext. 110. E. H. Aston, Libn.
Staff: 1 part time.
Size: 5,000 maps; 10 atlases.
Annual accessions: 250 maps; 2 atlases.
Subject specializations: topography; geology; oil and gas.
Serves: employees.
Interlibrary loan: not available.

La Jolla

40 UNIVERSITY OF CALIFORNIA, SCRIPPS INSTITUTION OF OCEANOGRAPHY, LIBRARY. (92037) Tel. 714/453-2000, ext. 1982. Cyril R. Gardner-Smith.
Staff: 1 part time.
Size: 33,000 maps; 500 atlases; 2 globes.
Annual accessions: 4,000 maps; 20 atlases.
Area specialization: oceans.
Subject specialization: hydrography; topography; geology.
Depository for: USGS (topo, geol).
Serves: Institution; public.
Interlibrary loan: not available.
Reproduction facility: Xerox.

Lodi

41 SAN JOAQUIN COUNTY HISTORICAL MUSEUM, P.O. Box 21. (95240) Tel. 209/368-9154. Mrs. Medora Johnson, Museum Director.

Staff: 2 part time.
Size: 300 maps.
Area specialization: San Joaquin County.
Special cartographic collection: old county plans and maps.
Serves: public.
Interlibrary loan: not available.

Long Beach

42 CALIFORNIA STATE COLLEGE AT LONG BEACH, DEPARTMENT OF GEOGRAPHY*, 6101 East Seventh Street. (90801) Tel. 213/433-0951.
Depository for: TOPOCOM.

43 CALIFORNIA STATE COLLEGE AT LONG BEACH, LIBRARY, SOCIAL SCIENCE REFERENCE DEPARTMENT, 6101 East Seventh Street. (90801) Tel. 213/433-0951, ext. 377.

Size: 3,250 maps; 160 atlases; 22 gazetteers.
Area specialization: California.
Depository for: California (State) Division of Mines and Geology.
Serves: College.
Interlibrary loan: not available.
Reproduction facilities: photocopy; Xerox.

Los Angeles

44 LOS ANGELES CITY COLLEGE, EARTH SCIENCE DEPARTMENT, 855 North Vermont Avenue. (90029) Tel. 213/663-9141, ext. 228. Arthur Carthew, Department Head.

Staff: 1 part time.
Size: 20,000 maps; 25 atlas folios; 10 globes; 50 relief models; 150 aerial photographs; 50 gazetteers.
Annual accessions: 500 maps; 10 relief models.
Area specialization: California.
Subject specializations: geography; geology.
Depository for: TOPOCOM; USGS (topo).
Serves: College.
Interlibrary loan: not available.
Reproduction facilities: photocopy; Xerox.

45 LOS ANGELES PUBLIC LIBRARY, 630 West 5th Street. (90017) Tel. 213/626-7461, ext. 311. Miss Karyle Butcher, Map Libn.

Staff: 2 full time.
Size: 71,252 maps; 1,150 atlases; 2 globes; 8 relief models.
Annual accessions: 2,078 maps; 50 atlases.
Area specializations: Los Angeles; California; western United States.
Subject specializations: topography; geology.
Special cartographic collections: Hulbert's *Crown Collection of Photographs of American Maps*; Los Angeles City maps dating from 1849.
Depository for: TOPOCOM; USGS (topo, geol).
Serves: public.
Interlibrary loan: available.

Reproduction facilities: photocopy; Xerox.
Publication: Maps in the Los Angeles Public Library.

46 UNIVERSITY OF CALIFORNIA AT LOS ANGELES, LIBRARY, DEPARTMENT OF SPECIAL COLLECTIONS. (90024) Tel. 213/825-4988. Evert Volkersz, Libn.
Staff: 1 part time.
Size: 1,800 maps; 75 atlases; 25 gazetteers.
Area specializations: western United States; pre-1900 southern California and Los Angeles.
Special cartographic collections: Stuart de Rothesay pamphlet maps (European coverage, 1785–1815); Robert E. Cowan Collection of California and the Pacific West; Shearman Collection of 17th and 18th century map makers.
Serves: University; public.
Interlibrary loan: not available.
Reproduction facilities: photocopy; Xerox; microfilm.

47 UNIVERSITY OF CALIFORNIA AT LOS ANGELES, MAP LIBRARY*, Room A-253. Social Sciences Building. (90024) Tel. 213/478-9711, ext. 7573. Carlos B. Hagen, Libn.
Size: 220,000 maps; 700 atlases; 11,000 aerial photographs.
Area specializations: Latin America; Africa; Pacific Ocean Basin.
Depository for: TOPOCOM.
Interlibrary loan: available.

Menlo Park

48 U.S. GEOLOGICAL SURVEY, LIBRARY, 345 Middlefield Road. (94025) Tel. 415/325-6761, ext. 208. Eleanore E. Wilkins, Libn.
Staff: 9 full time; 2 part time.
Size: 30,000 maps; 2 globes.
Annual accessions: 3,000 maps.
Area specialization: western United States.
Subject specializations: topography; geology.
Depository for: USGS (topo—western United States, geol).
Serves: employees; public.
Interlibrary loan: available.
Reproduction facility: Xerox.

Northridge

49 SAN FERNANDO VALLEY STATE COLLEGE, DEPARTMENT OF GEOGRAPHY, MAP LIBRARY, 18111 Nordhoff Street. (91324) Tel. 213/349-1200, ext. 715. Wallace C. St. Clair, Map Libn.
Staff: 1 full time; 3 part time.
Size: 165,000 maps; 50 atlases; 15 globes; 150 relief models; 5,500 aerial photographs; 35 gazetteers.
Subject specialization: topography.
Special cartographic collection: Sanborn insurance maps of United States cities.
Depository for: TOPOCOM; USGS (topo); Canada.
Serves: College; public.
Reproduction facilities: Xerox; Ozalid.

Oakland

50   OAKLAND PUBLIC LIBRARY, 125 14th Street. (94612) Tel. 415/444-8272, ext. 28. Gertrude M. Cordts, Libn.
Staff: 5 part time.
Size: 64,168 maps; 225 atlases; 3 globes; 5 relief models; 150 aerial photographs; 3 gazetteers.
Annual accessions: 5,768 maps; 12 atlases.
Area specializations: California; Alameda County.
Depository for: TOPOCOM; USGS (topo, geol–California).
Serves: public.
Interlibrary loan: available (restricted).
Reproduction facilities: photocopy; Xerox; microfilm.

Pasadena

51   CALIFORNIA INSTITUTE OF TECHNOLOGY, GEOLOGY DIVISION, MAP ROOM, 1201 East California Boulevard. (91109) Tel. 213/795-6841, ext. 2489.
Staff: 1 part time.
Size: not reported.
Area specializations: Canada; United States.
Subject specializations: geology; topography.
Depository for: USGS (topo, geol); Canada; Australia.
Serves: Institute; public.
Interlibrary loan: not available.
Reproduction facility: Xerox.

52   PASADENA PUBLIC LIBRARY, 285 East Walnut Street. (91101) Tel. 213/793-1151. Mrs. Jean T. Covalt, Libn.
Staff: 1 part time.
Size: 4,582 maps; 90 atlases; 1 globe; 7 gazetteers.
Annual accessions: 85 maps.
Area specialization: California.
Subject specializations: topography; history.
Depository for: USGS (topo—California).
Serves: public.
Interlibrary loan: not available.
Reproduction facility: photocopy.

Pleasant Hill

53   CONTRA COSTA COUNTY LIBRARY, DOCUMENTS SECTION, 1750 Oak Park Boulevard. (94523) Tel. 415/228-3000, ext. 296. Joseph Devere, Documents Libn.
Staff: 2 part time.
Size: 570 maps.
Annual accessions: 180 maps.
Area specialization: California.
Subject specializations: geology; topography.
Depository for: USGS (topo); California (State) Division of Mines and Geology.
Serves: public.
Interlibrary loan: not available.
Reproduction facility: Xerox.

Pomona

54 CALIFORNIA STATE POLYTECHNIC COLLEGE, LIBRARY, 3801 South Temple Avenue. (91766) Tel. 714/595-1241, ext. 450. Mai N. Shields, Reference Libn.
Size: 4,800 maps; 75 atlases.
Annual accessions: 250 maps.
Depository for: USGS (topo—western United States).
Serves: College; public.
Interlibrary loan: not available.
Reproduction facilities: photocopy; Xerox.

55 POMONA PUBLIC LIBRARY, 625 South Garey Avenue. (91766) Tel. 714/623-5211, ext. 25. Wayne Suggs, Map Libn.
Staff: 1 part time.
Size: 3,800 maps; 70 atlases; 1,000 aerial photographs; 5 gazetteers.
Area specialization: California.
Subject specializations: soils; topography.
Special collections: aerial photographs of Los Angeles and Orange counties; U.S. Soil Survey maps, 1905-1948.
Depository for: USGS (topo—California).
Serves: public.
Interlibrary loan: not available.
Reproduction facility: Xerox.

Port Hueneme

56 U.S. NAVAL CIVIL ENGINEERING LABORATORY, TECHNICAL LIBRARY DIVISION. (93041) Tel. 805/982-4252. Mrs. Hope S. Smith, Libn.
Staff: 1 part time.
Size: 954 maps; 6 atlases; 1 globe; 1 gazetteer.
Area specializations: western United States; Antarctica.
Subject specialization: oceanography.
Serves: employees.
Interlibrary loan: not available.
Reproduction facility: Xerox.

Riverside

57 RIVERSIDE PUBLIC LIBRARY, P.O. Box 468. (92502) Tel. 714/787-7376. Andrew D. Stephenson, Libn.
Staff: 1 part time.
Size: 1,000 maps; 55 atlases; 10 gazetteers.
Area specialization: southern California.
Depository for: California (State) Division of Mines and Geology (selective).
Serves: public.
Reproduction facility: Xerox.

58 UNIVERSITY OF CALIFORNIA AT RIVERSIDE, LIBRARY, MAP SECTION, P.O. Box 5900. (92507) Tel. 714/787-3233. Louise Burch, Library Assistant.
Staff: 2 full time; 2 part time.
Size: 45,255 maps; 500 atlases; 1 globe; 4 relief models; 150 gazetteers.
Annual accessions: 2,500 maps; 50 atlases.

Subject specialization: topography.
Depository for: TOPOCOM.
Serves: University.
Interlibrary loan: not available.
Reproduction facility: Xerox.

Sacramento

59 CALIFORNIA STATE ARCHIVES, 1020 O Street. (95814) Tel. 916/445-4293.
Size: 600 maps; 2,000 aerial photographs.
Annual accessions: 25 maps; 100 aerial photographs.
Subject specialization: California railroad route and roadbed maps.
Serves: public.
Interlibrary loan: not available.
Reproduction facilities: photocopy; Xerox; microfilm.

60 CALIFORNIA STATE LANDS COMMISSION, 1600 L Street. (95814) Tel. 916/445-6060. James Dorsey, Acting Supervisor, Land Records and Information Unit.
Staff: 2 part time.
Size: 5,000 maps; 10 atlases; 2 relief models; 3,000 aerial photographs.
Annual accessions: 200 maps; 200 aerial photographs.
Area specialization: California.
Subject specializations: hydrography; topography.
Special cartographic collections: maps of navigable water areas and public land cadastral surveys of California.
Serves: employees.
Interlibrary loan: not available.
Reproduction facilities: photocopy; Xerox; microfilm.

61 CALIFORNIA STATE LIBRARY, MAP ROOM. (95809) Tel. 916/445-5683. Mary Schell, Supervising Government Publications Libn.
Staff: 2 part time.
Size: 58,000 maps; 100 atlases; 2 globes; 50 relief models.
Annual accessions: 3,000 maps.
Area specializations: California state and county maps; United States.
Subject specialization: history.
Depository for: USGS (topo, geol).
Serves: public.
Interlibrary loan: not available.
Reproduction facility: photocopy.

62 SACRAMENTO STATE COLLEGE, 6000 Jay Street. (95819) Tel. 916/454-6144. John D. McClure III, Social Science and Business Administration Reference Libn.
Staff: 2 part time.
Size: 7,570 maps; 259 atlases; 37 relief models; 118 gazetteers.
Area specialization: California.
Depository for: USGS (topo—western United States).
Serves: College; public.
Interlibrary loan: not available.
Reproduction facility: Xerox.

San Bernardino

63 CALIFORNIA STATE COLLEGE AT SAN BERNARDINO, 5500 State College Parkway. (92407) Tel. 714/TU7-6311. Rosemary Ward, Map Libn.
Staff: 1 part time.
Size: 2,055 maps; 100 atlases; 1 globe; 1 relief model; 8 gazetteers.
Annual accessions: 200 maps; 10 atlases; 2 gazetteers.
Area specialization: California.
Subject specializations: topography; geology.
Serves: College; public.
Interlibrary loan: not available.
Reproduction facility: photocopy.

San Diego

64 SAN DIEGO PUBLIC LIBRARY, 820 E Street. (92119) Tel. 714/236-5800. Mr. Dalton Degitz, Libn.
Size: not reported.
Area specializations: San Diego City and County; Baja California; California.
Subject specializations: topography; geology.
Depository for: TOPOCOM; USGS (topo, geol).
Serves: public.
Interlibrary loan: not available.
Reproduction facilities: photocopy; Xerox.

65 SAN DIEGO STATE COLLEGE, DEPARTMENT OF GEOLOGY, 5402 College Avenue. (92115) Tel. 714/286-5589. Fred Brian, Technical Assistant.
Staff: 1 part time.
Size: 8,000 maps; 50 relief models; 1,000 aerial photographs.
Area specialization: California.
Subject specializations: topography; geology.
Depository for: USGS (topo, geol).
Serves: College.
Interlibrary loan: available.
Reproduction facilities: photocopy; Ozalid.

66 SAN DIEGO STATE COLLEGE, GEOGRAPHY DEPARTMENT, MAP LIBRARY. (92115) Tel. 714/286-5433. Mrs. Peggy A. Irish, Map Curator.
Staff: 1 full time.
Size: 80,000 maps; 75 atlases; 100 relief models; 2,000 aerial photographs; 50 gazetteers.
Annual accessions: 5,000 maps; 5 atlases; 20 relief models; 100 aerial photographs; 10 gazetteers.
Area specialization: California.
Subject specializations: topography; geology.
Special cartographic collection: daily weather maps for the United States and Canada.
Depository for: TOPOCOM; USGS (topo, geol).
Serves: College; public.
Publications: monthly acquisitions lists; map library brochure.

San Francisco

67 CALIFORNIA ACADEMY OF SCIENCES, LIBRARY, Golden Gate Park. (94118) Tel. 415/221-5100, ext. 75. Ray Brian, Libn.

Staff: 1 part time.
Size: 32,000 maps; 30 atlases; 20 gazetteers.
Area specialization: western United States.
Subject specializations: geology; hydrography; topography.
Depository for: TOPOCOM; USGS (topo, geol).
Serves: public.
Interlibrary loan: not available.

68   CALIFORNIA (STATE) DIVISION OF MINES AND GEOLOGY, LIBRARY, Ferry Building. (94111) Tel. 415/557-0308. Gary L. Ink, Libn.
Staff: 3 full time.
Size: 5,600 maps; 16 atlases; 6 relief models; 362 aerial photographs; 3 gazetteers.
Annual accessions: 150 maps.
Area specializations: western United States; California.
Subject specializations: topography; geology.
Special cartographic collection: geologic maps of the Soviet Union and Central Europe.
Depository for: USGS (topo); Canada; various states and foreign countries through exchange programs.
Serves: public.
Interlibrary loan: not available.
Reproduction facility: photocopy.

69   CALIFORNIA HISTORICAL SOCIETY, LIBRARY, 2090 Jackson Street. (94109) James de T. Abajian, Libn.
Staff: 1 part time.
Size: not reported.
Area specializations: western United States; California.
Serves: qualified researchers (upon approval).
Interlibrary loan: not available.

70   SAN FRANCISCO PUBLIC LIBRARY, CIVIC CENTER. (94102) Tel. 415/558-4927. Mrs. Karen Scannell, Libn., History Department.
Size: 33,000 maps; 330 wall maps; 260 atlases; 5 globes; 7 aerial photographs; 12 gazetteers.
Area specializations: San Francisco; California cities and counties; United States.
Subject specializations: local and state history; topography.
Depository for: USGS (topo).
Serves: public.
Reproduction facilities: Xerox; microfilm.

71   SAN FRANCISCO STATE COLLEGE, LIBRARY, SOCIAL SCIENCES AND BUSINESS LIBRARY*, 1630 Holloway Avenue. (94132) Tel. 415/469-1681. Hermine Sayer, Libn.
Depository for: TOPOCOM.

72   SIERRA CLUB, LIBRARY, Room 1050, Mills Tower, 220 Bush Street. (94104) Tel. 415/981-8634, ext. 41. Gordon Curtis, Libn.
Staff: 1 full time.
Size: 500 maps; 2 atlases; 1 globe; 1 relief model; 15 gazetteers.
Area specialization: Sierra Nevada.
Subject specialization: mountains and mountain ranges.
Serves: public.
Interlibrary loan: available.
Reproduction facility: Xerox.

73 SOCIETY OF CALIFORNIA PIONEERS, 456 McAllister. (94102) Tel. 415/861-5278. Mrs. Helen S. Giffen, Libn.
Size: not reported.
Area specializations: San Francisco; California counties and cities.
Subject specialization: local history.
Serves: public.
Interlibrary loan: not available.
Reproduction facility: photocopy.

74 STANDARD OIL COMPANY OF CALIFORNIA, GEOLOGY LIBRARY, Room 2265, 225 Bush Street. (94120) Tel. 415/434-7700, ext. 3270. Mrs. Margaret C. Marshburn, Geology Libn.
Staff: 1 part time.
Size: 3,500 maps; 15 atlases; 50 gazetteers.
Annual accessions: 60 maps.
Area specializations: California; Alaska.
Subject specializations: oil fields; oil and gas concessions.
Serves: employees; public (by permission).
Interlibrary loan: available.

San Marino

75 HENRY E. HUNTINGTON LIBRARY AND ART GALLERY. (91108) Tel. 213/792-6141. Herbert C. Schulz, Manuscript Collection; Carey S. Bliss, Prints Collection.
Size: 8,730 maps; 200 atlases; 6 globes.
Area specializations: England; United States.
Subject specialization: history.
Special collection: early sea charts.
Serves: qualified researchers (upon approval).
Interlibrary loan: not available.
Reproduction facilities: photocopy; Xerox; microfilm.
Publication: List of Early Maps and Charts, 1966, 13 pages. (unpublished, Xerox available, $6.00).

Santa Barbara

76 SANTA BARBARA MUSEUM OF NATURAL HISTORY, 2559 Puesta del Sol Road. (93105) Tel. 805/963-7821. Clifton Smith, Libn.
Staff: 1 full time.
Size: not reported.
Area specialization: Santa Barbara County.
Subject specialization: topography.
Depository for: USGS (topo, geol, selective).
Serves: public.

77 UNIVERSITY OF CALIFORNIA AT SANTA BARBARA, SCIENCES-ENGINEERING LIBRARY, MAP ROOM. (93106) Tel. 805/961-2779. Robert Sivers, Libn.
Staff: 3 full time; 3 part time.
Size: 63,657 maps; 386 atlases; 3 globes; 12,623 aerial photographs; 108 gazetteers.
Annual accessions: 10,000 maps; 30 atlases.
Area specializations: Africa; United States.
Depository for: USGS (topo, geol); USC&GS.

Serves: University; public.
Interlibrary loan: available.
Reproduction facility: Xerox.

Santa Cruz

78 UNIVERSITY OF CALIFORNIA AT SANTA CRUZ, UNIVERSITY
LIBRARY, MAP COLLECTION. (95060) Tel. 408/429-2364. Stanley D.
Stevens, Map Libn.
Staff: 1 full time; 8 part time.
Size: 7,500 maps; 4 globes; 50 relief models; 550 aerial photographs.
Annual accessions: 5,000 maps; 10 relief models.
Area specializations: Santa Cruz County; Monterey Bay area; Australia; New
Zealand; South Pacific.
Depository for: USGS (topo, geol).
Serves: University; public.
Interlibrary loan: available.
Reproduction facility: Xerox.
Publication: computer printed book catalog of the map collection.

Santa Monica

79 RAND CORPORATION, 1700 Main Street. (90406) Tel. 213/393-0411,
ext. 632.
Staff: 1 part time.
Size: 10,000 maps; 25 atlases; 120 gazetteers.
Serves: employees.
Interlibrary loan: not available.

80 SANTA MONICA PUBLIC LIBRARY, 1343 Sixth Street. (90401) Tel.
213/451-5751. Mrs. Martha Townsend, Head, Reference Department.
Staff: 1 part time.
Size: 2,993 maps; 40 atlases; 1 globe; 2 gazetteers.
Annual accessions: 200 maps; 3 atlases.
Area specialization: southern California.
Subject specialization: topography; geology.
Depository for: USGS (geol—California).
Serves: public.
Interlibrary loan: not available.
Reproduction facility: photocopy.

Stanford

81 STANFORD UNIVERSITY, LIBRARY, CENTRAL MAP COLLEC-
TION. (94305) Tel. 415/321-2300, ext. 2018. Miss Mary Louise Lee, Libn.
Staff: 1 full time; 1 part time.
Size: 80,075 maps.
Annual accessions: 1,000 maps.
Depository for: TOPOCOM.
Serves: University; public.
Interlibrary loan: available.
Reproduction facility: Xerox.

82 STANFORD UNIVERSITY, SCHOOL OF EARTH SCIENCES, BRAN-
NER GEOLOGICAL LIBRARY. (94305) Tel. 415/321-2300, ext. 2746.
Mrs. Kathryn N. Cutler, Head Libn.

Staff: 3 full time; 3 part time.
Size: 40,000 maps.
Annual accessions: 2,000 maps.
Area specialization: United States.
Subject specializations: geology; topography.
Depository for: USGS (topo, geol).
Serves: University; public.
Interlibrary loan: not available.
Reproduction facilities: photocopy; Xerox; microfilm.

Turlock

83 STANISLAUS STATE COLLEGE LIBRARY, 800 Monte Vista. (95380) Tel. 209/634-9101. J. Carlyle Parker, Head, Public Services.
Size: 1,156 maps; 44 atlases; 1 globe; 3 relief models; 11 gazetteers.
Area specialization: California.
Serves: College.
Reproduction facilities: Xerox; microfilm.

Whittier

84 WHITTIER COLLEGE, GEOLOGY DEPARTMENT. (90608) Tel. 213/693-0771, ext. 265. Dr. F. Beach Leighton.
Staff: 1 full time.
Size: 250,000 aerial photographs.
Area specialization: southern California.
Serves: College; public.
Interlibrary loan: not available.
Reproduction facility: Xerox.

CANAL ZONE

Balboa Heights

85 CANAL ZONE LIBRARY-MUSEUM, Box M. Tel. Balboa 4326. Mrs. Beverly Williams, Chief, Readers' Services.
Size: 250 maps; 5 relief models.
Area specialization: Isthmus of Panama.
Subject specializations: history and construction of the Panama Canal; canals.
Special cartographic collection: Garcia Collection—maps pertaining to the establishment of the Panama-Costa Rica boundary.
Serves: public.
Interlibrary loan: not available.
Reproduction facility: photocopy.

COLORADO

Boulder

86 UNIVERSITY OF COLORADO, MAP LIBRARY. (80302) Tel. 303/443-2211, ext. 7340. John Tull, Map Curator.
Staff: 2 part time.

Size: 70,000 maps; 10 atlases; 200 relief models.
Annual accessions: 3,000 maps.
Area specializations: North America.
Subject specialization: topography.
Depository for: TOPOCOM; USGS (topo).
Serves: University.
Interlibrary loan: not available.
Reproduction facilities: photocopy; Xerox; microfilm.

Colorado Springs

87 FOUNTAIN VALLEY SCHOOL, SCIENCE DEPARTMENT, MAP LIBRARY. (80911) Tel. 303/393-3641. F. Martin Brown, Head, Science Department.
Staff: 1 part time.
Size: 35,000 maps; 12 atlases; 24 relief models; 3,000 aerial photographs.
Annual accessions: 800 maps; 100 aerial photographs.
Area specializations: Colorado; southern Rocky Mountains.
Subject specializations: geomorphology; topography.
Depository for: TOPOCOM; USGS (topo–Colorado); Canada.
Serves: School; public.
Interlibrary loan: not available.
Reproduction facility: photocopy.

Denver

88 COLORADO (STATE) DEPARTMENT OF HIGHWAYS, LIBRARY, 4201 East Arkansas Avenue. (80222) Tel. 303/757-9308. Myrtle A. Swenson, Libn. (aerial photographs); Charles Mensing, Design Section (maps).
Size: 3,000 maps; 14,927 aerial photographs.
Annual accessions: 300 maps.
Area specialization: Colorado.
Subject specializations: highway engineering; urban geography; topography.
Serves: employees; public (by permission).
Interlibrary loan: not available.
Reproduction facilities: photocopy; Xerox; microfilm.

89 DENVER PUBLIC LIBRARY, 1357 Broadway. (80203) Tel. 303/266-0851.
Size: 25,448 maps; 713 atlases; 1 globe; 11 gazetteers.
Annual accessions: 2,650 maps.
Area specializations: western United States; North America.
Subject specializations: mining; exploration; railroads; land grants; topography; geology; history.
Special cartographic collections: early maps of western territories and United States; exploration maps listed in Warren's *Memoir* (1800–1857).
Depository for: TOPOCOM USGS (topo, geol).
Serves: public.
Interlibrary loan: not available.
Reproduction facilities: photocopy; Xerox.

90 JEPPESEN COMPANY, 8025 East 40th Avenue. (80207) Tel. 303/388-5301, ext. 266. Paul C. Rechel, Research Editor.
Staff: 2 part time.
Size: 3,971 maps; 17 atlases; 1 globe; 2 gazetteers.
Annual accessions: 580 maps; 2 atlases.

Area specializations: United States; South America; East Asia.
Subject specializations: airports; navigation; topography.
Special cartographic collection: airport obstruction and plan charts.
Serves: employees; public (by permission).
Interlibrary loan: not available.
Reproduction facility: Xerox.

91 STATE HISTORICAL SOCIETY OF COLORADO, LIBRARY, STATE MUSEUM, 200 14th Avenue. (80203) Tel. 303/892-2305. Mrs. Virginia Starkey.
Size: 1,625 maps.
Annual accessions: 125 maps.
Area specialization: Colorado.
Subject specializations: mining; city and town plats.
Special cartographic collection: Willard Map Collection.
Serves: public.
Interlibrary loan: not available.
Reproduction facilities: photocopy; Xerox.

92 U.S. GEOLOGICAL SURVEY, LIBRARY, Building 25, Denver Federal Center. (80225) Tel. 303/233-3611, ext.6733. Irvil P. Shultz, Libn.
Staff: 2 part time.
Size: 50,000 maps; 100 atlases; 2 globes; 80 gazetteers.
Annual accessions: 1,000 maps.
Area specialization: United States.
Subject specializations: geology; topography.
Depository for: USGS (topo, geol).
Serves: public.
Interlibrary loan: available.
Reproduction facility: Denison copier.

93 UNIVERSITY OF DENVER, DEPARTMENT OF GEOGRAPHY. (80210) Tel. 303/753-2513. Dr. Laurance C. Herold, Associate Professor.
Staff: 1 part time.
Size: 20,000 maps; 30 atlases; 4 globes; 200 relief models; 1,000 aerial photographs; 87 gazetteers.
Annual accessions: 1,000 maps; 5 atlases; 100 aerial photographs; 6 gazetteers.
Depository for: TOPOCOM.
Serves: University.
Interlibrary loan: not available.

Fort Collins

94 COLORADO STATE UNIVERSITY, LIBRARY. (80521) Tel. 303/491-6626. Mrs. Betty L. Hacker, Social Sciences Libn.
Staff: 2 part time.
Size: 6,000 maps; 300 atlases.
Annual accessions: 1,000 maps; 50 atlases.
Area specialization: western United States.
Subject specialization: topography; geology.
Depository for: USGS (topo, geol).
Serves: University.
Interlibrary loan: available.
Reproduction facilities: photocopy; Xerox.

Golden

95 COLORADO SCHOOL OF MINES, LIBRARY*. (80401) Tel. 303/279-3381, ext. 364.

Size: 55,500 maps.
Subject specializations: geology; topography.
Depository for: TOPOCOM; USGS (topo, geol).

Gunnison

96 WESTERN STATE COLLEGE, GEOLOGY DEPARTMENT. (81230) Tel. 303/943-2092. Dr. Thomas L. Prather, Associate Professor of Geology.

Staff: 1 part time.
Size: not reported.
Area specialization: western United States.
Subject specializations: topography; geology.
Depository for: USGS (topo, geol).
Serves: College; public.
Interlibrary loan: not available.
Reproduction facilities: photocopy; Xerox.

Littleton

97 MARATHON OIL COMPANY, DENVER RESEARCH CENTER LIBRARY, P.O. Box 269. (80120) Tel. 303/794-2601, ext. 276. Clarence A. Sturdivant, Supervisor, Technical Information.

Staff: 3 full time; 2 part time.
Size: 6,000 maps; 50 atlases; 1 globe; 100 aerial photographs; 10 gazetteers.
Annual accessions: 500 maps; 5 atlases; 10 aerial photographs; 3 gazetteers.
Area specialization: Western Hemisphere.
Subject specializations: geology; oil and gas.
Serves: employees; public (by permission).
Interlibrary loan: available.
Reproduction facility: Xerox.

U.S. Air Force Academy

98 U.S. AIR FORCE ACADEMY, LIBRARY. (80840) Tel. 303/472-4774. Mrs. Harriet Romberger.

Staff: 1 part time.
Size: 13,314 maps; 282 atlases; 2 globes; 86 relief models; 171 aerial photographs; 125 gazetteers.
Annual accessions: 1,700 maps.
Area specialization: Moon.
Serves: Academy.
Interlibrary loan: available.
Reproduction facilities: photocopy; Xerox.

CONNECTICUT

Bridgeport

99 BRIDGEPORT PUBLIC LIBRARY, 925 Broad Street. (06605) Tel. 203/333-8551, ext. 421.

Size: not reported.
Area specializations: Bridgeport; Connecticut.
Subject specializations: geology; local history.
Depository for: USGS (geol).
Serves: public.
Interlibrary loan: not available.
Reproduction facility: Docustat.

Hartford

100   CONNECTICUT HISTORICAL SOCIETY, 1 Elizabeth Street. (06105)
Tel. 203/236-5622. M.W. Jacobus, Curator of Prints.
Staff: 1 part time.
Size: 441 maps; 62 atlases; 4 globes; 1,354 aerial photographs; 4 gazetteers.
Area specialization: Connecticut.
Serves: public.
Interlibrary loan: not available.
Publications: significant accessions are listed in the Connecticut Historical Society
quarterly bulletins and annual reports.

101   CONNECTICUT STATE LIBRARY, HISTORY AND GENEALOGY
SECTION, 231 Capitol Avenue. (06115) Tel. 203/527-6341, ext. 2167. Mrs.
Janet H. Axman, Section Head.
Size: 1,800 maps; 400 atlases; 4 globes; 10 relief models; 180 gazetteers.
Area specialization: Connecticut.
Subject specializations: local history; topography; urban geography.
Serves: public.
Interlibrary loan: not available.
Reproduction facilities: photocopy, Xerox.

102   HARTFORD PUBLIC LIBRARY, 500 Main Street. (06103) Tel. 203/525-
9121. Miss Josephine W. Sale, Head, Reference and General Reading
Department.
Size: 32,000 maps.
Annual accessions: 200 maps.
Area specializations: Hartford; Connecticut.
Depository for: TOPOCOM; USGS (topo—New England).
Serves: public.
Interlibrary loan: available.
Reproduction facility: Xerox.

103   TRINITY COLLEGE, WATKINSON LIBRARY. (06106) Tel. 203/527-
3153. ext. 307. Mrs. Marian Clarke, Curator.
Size: 550 maps; 100 atlases; 25 gazetteers.
Area specialization: eastern United States.
Subject specialization: discovery and exploration.
Serves: College; public.
Interlibrary loan: not available.
Reproduction facilities: photocopy; Xerox; microfilm.

Middletown

104   WESLEYAN UNIVERSITY, GEOLOGY LIBRARY*. (06457) Tel. 203/
347-4421, ext. 282.
Depository for: TOPOCOM.

Mystic

105 MYSTIC SEAPORT, G. W. BLUNT WHITE LIBRARY. (06355) Tel. 203/ 536-2631. Mrs. Virginia Allen, Custodian of Charts.
Staff: 1 part time.
Size: 2,000 charts.
Subject specialization: navigation.
Serves: public.
Interlibrary loan: not available.

New Britain

106 CENTRAL CONNECTICUT STATE COLLEGE, DEPARTMENT OF SOCIAL SCIENCES*, 1615 Stanley Street. (06050).
Depository for: TOPOCOM.

New Haven

107 YALE UNIVERSITY, GEOLOGY LIBRARY, Box 2161 Yale Station. (06520) Tel. 203/787-3131, ext. 487. Harry D. Scammell, Libn.
Staff: 3 full time; 1 part time.
Size: 60,000 maps.
Annual accessions: 2,000 maps.
Subject specializations: geology; topography.
Depository for: USGS (topo, geol); Canada.
Serves: University.
Reproduction facilities: Xerox; Ozalid.

108 YALE UNIVERSITY, LIBRARY, MAP COLLECTION, Box 1603A Yale Station. (06520) Tel. 203/787-3131, ext. 2495. Alexander Orr Vietor, Curator of Maps.
Staff: 2 full time; 2 part time.
Size: 150,000 maps; 2,250 atlases; 15 globes.
Annual accessions: 1,500 maps; 100 atlases.
Area specializations: United States; New England; Great Britain.
Subject specializations: historical cartography; topography.
Special cartographic collections: Portolan charts of early dates (15th and 16th centuries); early navigation charts.
Depository for: TOPOCOM; USGS (topo); Canada.
Serves: University; public.
Interlibrary loan: available.
Reproduction facilities: photocopy; Xerox; microfilm.

Storrs

109 UNIVERSITY OF CONNECTICUT, WILBER CROSS LIBRARY. (06268) Tel. 203/429-3311, ext. 884. R.H. Schimmelpfeng, Director, Special Collections.
Staff: 1 full time.
Size: 60,000 maps; 15 atlases; 31 gazetteers.
Annual accessions: 10,000 maps.
Subject specializations: topography; geology.
Depository for: TOPOCOM; USGS (topo, geol).
Serves: University; public.
Interlibrary loan: available.
Reproduction facility: Xerox.

DELAWARE

Dover

110 DELAWARE STATE ARCHIVES, Hall of Records. (19901) Tel. 302/734-5711, ext. 256 or 257. Leon deValinger, Jr., State Archivist.
Staff: 2 part time.
Size: 300 maps; 8 atlases; 30 relief models.
Annual accessions: 10 maps.
Area specialization: Delaware.
Serves: public.
Interlibrary loan: not available.
Reproduction facilities: photocopy; microfilm.

Newark

111 UNIVERSITY OF DELAWARE, MORRIS LIBRARY, MAP LIBRARY. (19711) Tel. 302/738-2238. Charles W. Mason, Documents Libn.
Staff: 3 full time; 2 part time.
Size: 44,000 maps; 247 atlases; 1 globe, 10 volumes of aerial photographs; 127 gazetteers.
Annual accessions: 2,818 maps.
Area specializations: United States; Moon.
Subject specializations: geology; climatology; natural resources.
Depository for: TOPOCOM; USGS (topo, geol); USC&GS.
Serves: University; public.
Interlibrary loan: not available.
Reproduction facility: Xerox.

Wilmington

112 HISTORICAL SOCIETY OF DELAWARE, 509 Market Street. (19801) Tel. 302/658-9432. Mrs. Gladys Coghlan.
Staff: 2 part time.
Size: 800 maps; 35 atlases.
Area specialization: Delaware.
Subject specialization: geography.
Serves: public.
Interlibrary loan: not available.
Reproduction facilities: photocopy; Xerox.

113 WILMINGTON INSTITUTE FREE LIBRARY, 10th and Market Streets. (19801) Tel. 302/656-3131. Christopher B. Devan, Director.
Staff: 1 part time.
Size: 28,557 maps; 53 atlases; 1 globe.
Area specialization: Delaware.
Subject specializations: history; topography.
Depository for: USGS (topo).
Serves: public.
Interlibrary loan: not available.
Reproduction facility: photocopy.

DISTRICT OF COLUMBIA

114 AMERICAN AUTOMOBILE ASSOCIATION, LIBRARY, 1712 G Street, N.W. (20006) Tel. 202/638-4000, ext. 494. Mrs. Sue Williams, Libn.
Size: 1,000 maps; 5 atlases; 1 gazetteer.
Annual accessions: 50 maps.
Area specializations: United States; Canada; Mexico.
Subject specialization: road maps.
Serves: employees; public.
Interlibrary loan: available.
Reproduction facility: Xerox.

115 CATHOLIC UNIVERSITY OF AMERICA, MAP LIBRARY. (20017) Tel. 202/LA9-6000, ext. 259. Dr. Kenneth J. Bertrand, Head, Geography Department.
Staff: 1 part time.
Size: 25,000 maps; 125 atlases; 4 globes; 10 relief models; 1,700 aerial photographs.
Annual accessions: 400 maps; 10 atlases; 100 aerial photographs.
Area specialization: United States.
Subject specializations: geology; topography.
Depository for: TOPOCOM; USGS (topo, geol).
Serves: University.
Interlibrary loan: not available.
Reproduction facilities: photocopy; Xerox; microfilm.

116 GEORGE WASHINGTON UNIVERSITY, LIBRARY*, 2023 G Street, N.W. (20006) Tel. 202/676-6840.
Depository for: TOPOCOM.

117 METROPOLITAN WASHINGTON COUNCIL OF GOVERNMENTS, GRAPHIC ARTS SECTION, 1225 Connecticut Avenue, N.W. (20036) Tel. 202/223-6800, ext. 288 or 289. Charles Saberin, Chief.
Staff: 1 part time.
Size: 2,000 maps.
Annual accessions: 300 maps.
Area specialization: Washington, D.C. and vicinity.
Subject specializations: land use; transportation.
Serves: employees; Council members; public (by permission).
Interlibrary loan: not available.
Reproduction facility: Diazo.

118 NATIONAL CAPITAL PLANNING COMMISSION, 726 Jackson Place, N.W. (20576) Tel. 202/382-1895. Francis H. Deter, Jr., Chief, Cartography and Drafting Services.
Staff: 5 full time.
Size: 26,000 maps; 14 atlases; 600 aerial photographs.
Annual accessions: 1,000 maps; 50 aerial photographs.
Area specialization: Washington, D.C. and vicinity.
Subject specializations: urban planning; transportation; parks and recreation.
Depository for: USGS (topo).
Serves: employees, public.
Interlibrary loan: available (restricted).
Reproduction facilities: Xerox; microfilm; Ozalid; Diazo.

119 NATIONAL GEOGRAPHIC SOCIETY, MAP LIBRARY, 17th and M Streets, N.W. (20036) Tel. 202/296-7500, ext. 787. Dennis M. Sheffield, Map Libn.
Staff: 2 full time.
Size: 72,200 maps; 401 atlases; 95 relief models; 174 aerial photographs; 250 gazetteers.
Annual accessions: 3,000 maps; 35 atlases; 25 relief models; 15 gazetteers.
Depository for: TOPOCOM; USGS (topo).
Serves: employees.
Interlibrary loan: available.

120 PAN AMERICAN UNION, COLUMBUS MEMORIAL LIBRARY. (20006) Tel. 202/DU 1-8254. Arthur E. Gropp, Libn.
Size: 3,000 maps.
Area specialization: Latin America.
Serves: employees; public.
Interlibrary loan: not available.

121 PUBLIC LIBRARY OF THE DISTRICT OF COLUMBIA, CENTRAL LIBRARY, HISTORY, GEOGRAPHY, AND GOVERNMENT DIVISION, 8th and K Streets, N.W. (20001) Tel. 202/NA 8-6776. Miss Eleanor A. Bartlett, Chief.
Size: 3,691 maps; 210 atlases; 2 globes; 2 relief models.
Annual accessions: 100 maps; 10 atlases.
Depository for: USGS (topo—Middle Atlantic states).
Serves: public.
Interlibrary loan: available (restricted).
Reproduction facility: Dennison copier.

122 PUBLIC LIBRARY OF THE DISTRICT OF COLUMBIA, CENTRAL LIBRARY, WASHINGTONIANA DIVISION, 8th and K Streets, N.W. (20001) Tel. 202/ NA 8-6776. Miss Sue Shivers, Chief.
Staff: 2 part time.
Size: 648 maps; 95 atlases.
Annual accessions: 5 maps.
Area specialization: Washington, D.C.
Subject specialization: local history.
Serves: public.
Interlibrary loan: not available.
Reproduction facility: Dennison copier.

123 PUBLIC LIBRARY OF THE DISTRICT OF COLUMBIA, GEORGETOWN BRANCH, Wisconsin Avenue and R Street, N.W. Tel. 202/565-2268.
Special cartographic collection: Peabody Library Association collection of early Georgetown maps.
Serves: public.

124 U.S. ARMY TOPOGRAPHIC COMMAND, 6500 Brooks Lane. (20315) Tel. 301/986-2307. Frank T. Nicoletti, Chief, Information Resources Division.
Staff: 150 full time.
Size: 1,600,000 maps.
Annual accessions: 75,000 maps.

Area specializations: comprehensive.
Subject specializations: topography; transportation; political and physical geography; communications.
Serves: Federal agencies and employees.
Reproduction facilities: photocopy; Xerox; microfilm.
Publications: periodic accessions lists.

125 U.S. BUREAU OF THE CENSUS, GEOGRAPHY DIVISION. (20233) Tel. 301/440-7007. Robert L. Hagan, Assistant Chief for Planning.
Staff: 2 full time; 2 part time.
Size: 400,000 maps.
Area specialization: United States.
Subject specialization: topography.
Depository for: USGS (topo).
Serves: employees.
Interlibrary loan: not available.
Reproduction facilities: photocopy; Xerox; microfilm.

126 U.S. DEPARTMENT OF THE NAVY, LIBRARY, Room 1241, Main Navy Building. (20360) Tel. 202/OX 6-1772. Miss Mary F. Pickens.
Staff: 1 part time.
Size: 3,000 maps; 10 atlases.
Annual accessions: 300 maps; 5 atlases.
Area specializations: eastern North America; West Indies; western Europe.
Subject specialization: naval and maritime aspects of the American Revolution.
Serves: employees; public (by permission).
Reproduction facilities: photocopy; Xerox; microfilm.

127 U.S. FEDERAL HIGHWAY ADMINISTRATION, CARTOGRAPHIC SECTION, 1717 H Street, N.W. (20591) Tel. 202/967-2081. Edward L. Poland.
Staff: 1 full time.
Size: 75,000 maps.
Annual accessions: 1,500 maps.
Area specialization: United States.
Subject specializations: transportation; topography; urban geography.
Serves: employees; public.
Reproduction facility: Xerox.

128 U.S. GEOLOGICAL SURVEY, LIBRARY, Room 1033, GSA Building, 19th and F Streets, N.W. (20242) Tel. 202/343-3864. Mark W. Pangborn, Jr., Map Curator.
Staff: 3 full time; 2 part time.
Size: 100,000 maps; 500 atlases; 1,000 gazetteers.
Annual accessions: 6,000 maps; 10 atlases; 20 gazetteers.
Area specialization: comprehensive.
Subject specializations: mineral resources; soils; water resources; topography; geology.
Depository for: USGS (topo, geol).
Serves: employees; public.
Interlibrary loan: available.

129 U.S. LIBRARY OF CONGRESS, GEOGRAPHY AND MAP DIVISION. (20540) Tel. 703/370-1216. Dr. Walter W. Ristow, Chief.

Staff: 30 full time.

Size: 3,350,000 maps; 30,500 atlases; 500 globes; 500 relief models.

Annual accessions: 130,000 maps; 2,200 atlases; 6 globes; 25 relief models.

Area specializations: comprehensive worldwide; United States.

Subject specializations: comprehensive; history.

Special cartographic collections: Montgomery Blair Collection of 19th century maps; William Faden Collection of French and Indian and Revolutionary War maps; Millard Fillmore Collection of 19th Century maps; Jedediah Hotchkiss Collection of Confederate Civil War maps; Admiral Lord Richard Howe Collection of 18th century maps; Johann Georg Kohl manuscript copies of early maps of America; Woodbury Lowery Collection of maps of Spanish possessions in America 1502–1820; Oriental Collection of rare manuscript and printed maps and atlases; Ozanne Collection of manuscript views and maps of the Revolutionary War; Portolan charts and atlases of the 15th–17th centuries; Comte de Rochambeau Collection of Revolutionary War maps; William T. Sherman Collection of Civil War maps; Ephraim G. Squier Collection of maps of Central America.

Depository for: all major national and foreign mapping agencies, official and commercial.

Serves: Congress; Federal agencies; staff; public.

Interlibrary loan: available (restricted).

Reproduction facilities: photocopy; Xerox; microfilm.

Publications: Facsimiles of Rare Historical Maps; The Geography and Map Division of the Library of Congress (information brochure); Aviation Cartography; A Guide to Historical Cartography; John Smith Map of Virginia, 1612 (facsimile, with descriptive text); Selected Maps and Charts of Antarctica; United States Atlases (2 v.); A List of Maps of America (o.p.); A List of Geographical Atlases (6 v.; v. 1–4 o.p.); The Lowery Collection (o.p.); Maps, Their Care, Repair and Preservation in Libraries (o.p.); Marketing Maps of the United States (o.p.); Civil War Maps; A Descriptive List of Treasure Maps and Charts; Maps Showing Explorers' Routes, Trails and Early Roads in the United States; Three-Dimensional Maps; Land Ownership Maps; Detroit and Vicinity before 1900; The Hotchkiss Map Collection (o.p.).

130 U.S. NATIONAL ARCHIVES AND RECORDS SERVICE, CARTO-GRAPHIC BRANCH, 8th and Pennsylvania Avenue, N.W. (20408) Tel. 202/962-3181. Dr. Philip Muntz, Chief.

Staff: 11 full time.

Size: 1,500,000 maps; 2,250,000 aerial photographs.

Annual accessions: 25,000 maps.

Area specializations: comprehensive; United States.

Subject specialization: historical geography of the United States.

Depository for: TOPOCOM; USGS (topo, geol); other Federal mapping agencies.

Serves: employees; public.

Interlibrary loan: not available.

Reproduction facilities: photocopy; Xerox; microfilm.

Publications: PRELIMINARY INVENTORIES—Cartographic Records of the Federal Housing Administration (o.p.); Cartographic Records of the American Commission to Negotiate Peace (o.p.); Cartographic Records of the United States Marine Corps (o.p.); Cartographic Records of the Office of the Secretary of the Interior (o.p.); Cartographic Records of the Chief of Naval Operations; Cartographic Records of the Panama Canal; Cartographic Records of the Bureau of the Census; Cartographic Records of the American Expeditionary

Forces, 1917–21; Cartographic Records of the Forest Service; SPECIAL LISTS— *List of Cartographic Records of the Bureau of Indian Affairs; List of Cartographic Records of the General Land Office;* GENERAL FINDING AIDS— *Civil War Maps in the National Archives;* MISCELLANEOUS PUBLICATIONS—*Geographic Exploration and Topographic Mapping by the Unites States Government: A Catalog; United States Scientific Geographical Exploration of the Pacific Basin; Federal Exploration of the American West Before 1880.*
Note: This agency is the official repository for permanently valuable non-current records of the Federal Government.

131   U.S. NAVAL OCEANOGRAPHIC OFFICE, NAUTICAL CHART LIBRARY. (20390) Tel. 301/763-1038. Kells M. Boland, Head.
Staff: 8 full time.
Size: 62,000 charts.
Annual accessions: 3,600 maps.
Area specialization: comprehensive.
Subject specializations: ocean; coastal and harbor charts; intra-coastal waterways; port plans; bathymetry.
Serves: authorized Federal agencies; others by approved advance request.
Interlibrary loan: available (restricted).
Reproduction facilities: photocopy; Xerox.
Publications: Biannual Catalog; Monthly Accessions List; computer data printouts. Distribution limited to authorized agencies only.
Note: An integral part of the Library is its Automated Nautical Chart Information File (ANCIF). This automated system enables the Library to provide computer generated periodic lists of library holdings, and to furnish data quickly and accurately when needed.

132   U.S. POST OFFICE DEPARTMENT, LIBRARY, 12th Street and Pennsylvania Avenue, N.W. (20260) Tel. 202/961-7588. Gertrude Enders, Reference Libn.
Size: 1,973 maps; 31 atlases; 3 gazetteers.
Annual accessions: 75 maps.
Area specialization: United States.
Subject specialization: post routes.
Serves: employees; public.
Interlibrary loan: available.
Reproduction facility: photocopy.

FLORIDA

Boca Raton

133   FLORIDA ATLANTIC UNIVERSITY, LIBRARY*. (33432) Tel. 305/395-5705.
Depository for: TOPOCOM.

Coral Gables

134   UNIVERSITY OF MIAMI, GEOGRAPHY DEPARTMENT, MAP LIBRARY, Box 8152. (33124) Tel. 305/284-4087. Dr. Richard D. Kreske, Professor.
Staff: 4 part time.

Size: 48,000 maps; 200 atlases; 40 globes; 40 relief models; 6,000 aerial photographs; 40 gazetteers.
Annual accessions: 3,000 maps; 10 atlases; 1,000 aerial photographs.
Depository for: TOPOCOM.
Serves: University; public.
Interlibrary loan: not available.
Reproduction facility: photocopy.

Gainesville

135 UNIVERSITY OF FLORIDA, P.K. YONGE LIBRARY OF FLORIDA HISTORY. (32601) Tel. 904/392-0319. Elizabeth Alexander, Libn.
Staff: 2 full time.
Size: 850 maps.
Annual accessions: 50 maps.
Area specializations: Florida; southeastern United States.
Subject specialization: local history.
Serves: University; public.
Interlibrary loan: not available.
Reproduction facilities: photocopy; Xerox; microfilm.

136 UNIVERSITY OF FLORIDA, UNIVERSITY LIBRARY, MAP ROOM. (32601) Tel. 904/376-3261, ext. 2321. Miss Lillian Seaberg, Assistant Libn.
Staff: 3 part time.
Size: 125,000 maps; 150 atlases; 1 globe; 367 gazetteers.
Annual accessions: 3,000 maps.
Depository for: TOPOCOM; USGS (topo, geol).
Serves: University; public.
Interlibrary loan: not available.
Reproduction facility: Xerox.

Lake Alfred

137 CITRUS EXPERIMENT STATION, LIBRARY, P.O. Box 1088 (33850) Tel. 813/372-1151, ext.226. Pamela K. Hearon, Assistant Libn.
Size: 800 maps; 1 atlas.
Annual accessions: 15 maps.
Area specialization: Florida.
Depository for: USGS (geol).
Serves: staff; public.
Interlibrary loan: not available.
Reproduction facility: Xerox.

Pensacola

138 UNIVERSITY OF WEST FLORIDA, LIBRARY. (32504) Tel. 904/476-9500, ext. 261. Marion Viccars, Assistant Libn.
Staff: 1 part time.
Size: 877 maps; 36 atlases; 1 globe; 20 aerial photographs.
Area specializations: Florida; southeastern United States.
Serves: University; public.
Interlibrary loan: available.
Reproduction facilities: photocopy; Xerox.

Tallahassee

139 FLORIDA (STATE) BOARD OF CONSERVATION, DIVISION OF GEOLOGY, LIBRARY, P.O. Box 631. (32302) Tel. 904/224-7141, ext. 295. Caroline N. Choate, Libn.
Staff: 1 full time; 1 part time.
Size: 10,000 maps; 30 atlases; 600 aerial photographs; 1 gazetteer.
Annual accessions: 300 maps.
Area specializations: Florida; United States.
Subject specializations: hydrography; topography; geology.
Depository for: USGS (topo, geol); USC&GS (nautical charts).
Serves: employees; public.
Interlibrary loan: available.
Reproduction facility: Xerox.

140 FLORIDA STATE UNIVERSITY, STROZIER LIBRARY, MAP SECTION. (32306) Tel. 904/599-2015. Marianne Donnell, Map Libn.
Staff: 1 full time; 3 part time.
Size: 76,000 maps; 760 atlases; 11 globes; 6 relief models; 5 gazetteers.
Annual accessions: 2,600 maps.
Area specializations: Florida; southeastern United States.
Subject specializations: history; topography; geology.
Special collections: Matthews Collection (202 sheets); Dr. Mark Boyd Collection (52 sheets).
Depository for: TOPOCOM; USGS (topo, geol).
Serves: University; public.
Interlibrary loan: available.
Reproduction facilities: Xerox; microfilm.

Tampa

141 UNIVERSITY OF SOUTH FLORIDA, LIBRARY*. (33620) Tel. 813/988-4131.
Depository for: TOPOCOM.

Winter Park

142 Rollins College, Mills Memorial Library. (32789) Tel. 305/646-2000, ext. 2376. Margaret D. Duer, Assistant Reference Libn.
Staff: 1 part time.
Size: 7,492 maps; 50 atlases; 3 globes; 3 relief models.
Annual accessions: 50 maps.
Area specialization: Latin America.
Special collection: Frederic Boyer Collection.
Depository for: USGS (topo, geol).
Serves: College; public.
Interlibrary loan: available.
Reproduction facility: Xerox.

GEORGIA

Athens

143 UNIVERSITY OF GEORGIA, LIBRARY, SCIENCE LIBRARY, MAP COLLECTION. (30601) Tel. 404/542-4535. Miss Ann Ray Hogin, Map Libn.

Staff: 1 full time.
Size: 175,000 maps; 100 atlases; 74,475 aerial photographs; 40 gazetteers.
Annual accessions: 5,000 maps.
Area specialization: southeastern United States.
Subject specializations: geology; topography.
Depository for: TOPOCOM; USGS (topo, geol).
Serves: University.
Interlibrary loan: available.
Reproduction facilities: photocopy; Xerox.
Publications: University of Georgia Map Library Selected Acquisitions (quarterly).

144 UNIVERSITY OF GEORGIA, LIBRARY, SPECIAL COLLECTIONS, Room 315. (30601) Tel. 404/542-2972. John W. Bonner, Jr., Special Collections Libn.
Size: 661 maps.
Area specializations: Georgia; southeastern United States.
Subject specialization: local history.
Serves: University; public.
Interlibrary loan: not available.
Reproduction facilities: photocopy; Xerox; microfilm.

Atlanta

145 ATLANTA HISTORICAL SOCIETY, P.O. Box 12423. (30305) Tel. 404/261-6055. Mrs. Dorris Douglass, Libn.
Staff: 2 full time.
Size: not reported.
Area specializations: Atlanta; Fulton County; Georgia.
Serves: public.
Interlibrary loan: not available.
Reproduction facility: Xerox.

146 GEORGIA INSTITUTE OF TECHNOLOGY, PRICE GILBERT MEMORIAL LIBRARY. (30332) Tel. 404/873-4211, ext. 673. Miss Safford Harris, Special Collections Libn.
Staff: 1 part time.
Size: 52,141 maps; 579 atlases; 2 globes; 71 relief models; 594 aerial photographs; 118 gazetteers.
Annual accessions: 3,207 maps; 10 atlases; 10 relief models; 10 aerial photographs.
Area specializations: Georgia; southeastern United States.
Subject specializations: transportation; city planning; architecture; topography; geology.
Special cartographic collection: Joan Blaeu *Grooten Atlas,* Dutch text, 9 volumes.
Depository for: TOPOCOM; USGS (topo, geol).
Serves: students; public.
Interlibrary loan: available.
Reproduction facilities: photocopy, Xerox; microfilm.

147 GEORGIA (STATE) SURVEYOR GENERAL DEPARTMENT, CARTOGRAPHIC COLLECTION, Archives and Records Building. (30334) Tel. 404/522-0010, ext. 248. Mrs. Philip W. Bryant, Deputy Surveyor General.
Staff: 2 full time.
Size: 1,200 maps; 12 atlases; 10 relief models; 3 gazetteers.
Annual accessions: 100 maps.
Area specializations: Georgia; southeastern United States.

Subject specialization: Surveys of land districts in Georgia.
Special cartographic collection: Dr. John H. Goff Collection of southern place names, Indian trails, towns, forts, and ferries.
Depository for: USGS (topo—Georgia).
Serves: staff; public.
Interlibrary loan: not available.
Reproduction facilities: photocopy; Xerox; microfilm.

Douglas

148 SOUTH GEORGIA COLLEGE, WILLIAM S. SMITH LIBRARY. (31533) Tel. 912/384-1100, ext. 250. Mrs. Winifred Smith.
Staff: 1 part time.
Size: 5,526 maps; 45 atlases; 580 relief models; 17 gazetteers.
Annual accessions: 3,000 maps; 5 atlases; 300 aerial photographs.
Depository for: USGS (topo).
Serves: College; public.
Interlibrary loan: not available.
Reproduction facility: Xerox.

Savannah

149 GEORGIA HISTORICAL SOCIETY, 501 Whitaker Street. (31401) Tel. 912/234-1585. Mrs. Lilla M. Hawes, Director.
Size: 616 maps; 22 atlases; 14 gazetteers.
Annual accessions: 130 maps.
Area specializations: Savannah and Chatham County, Georgia; southeastern United States.
Depository for: USGS (geol—southeastern States).
Serves: public.
Interlibrary loan: not available.
Reproduction facilities: commercial facilities available locally.

HAWAII

Hilo

150 UNIVERSITY OF HAWAII, HILO CAMPUS, P.O. Box 1357. (96720) Tel. 808/935-2821, ext. 123. Mrs. Junko Ida Nowaki, Assistant Libn.
Size: 300 maps; 20 atlases; 1 globe; 15 gazetteers.
Annual accessions: 10 maps; 4 atlases; 3 gazetteers.
Area specialization: Hawaii.
Serves: University; public.
Interlibrary loan: available.

Honolulu

151 BERNICE P. BISHOP MUSEUM, PACIFIC SCIENTIFIC INFORMATION CENTER, WATERHOUSE MAP ROOM. (98619) Tel. 808/85-5951. Edwin H. Bryan, Jr., Manager.
Staff: 3 part time.
Size: 12,000 maps; 12 atlases; 3 relief models; 65,000 aerial photographs; 120 gazetteers.
Annual accessions: 150 maps.

Area specializations: Pacific Basin; Australasia; southeastern Asia.
Subject specializations: hydrography; topography; biogeography.
Serves: public.
Interlibrary loan: not available.
Reproduction facilities: photocopy; Xerox.

152   HAWAII STATE ARCHIVES, Iolani Palace Grounds. (96813) Mrs. Jane Azama, Archivist.
Staff: 1 part time.
Size: 350 maps; 1,000 aerial photographs.
Annual accessions: 15 maps.
Area specialization: Hawaii.
Serves: public.
Interlibrary loan: not available.
Reproduction facility: photocopy.

153   HAWAII STATE LIBRARY, 478 South King Street. (96813) Tel. 808/533-6081. Mrs. Donna M. Garcia, Director.
Size: 1,852 maps; 2 globes; 1 relief model.
Area specializations: Hawaii; Pacific Ocean.
Subject specializations: history; travel.
Serves: public.
Interlibrary loan: available.
Reproduction facility: Xerox.

154   UNIVERSITY OF HAWAII, GRADUATE RESEARCH LIBRARY, SOCIAL SCIENCE BRANCH, MAP COLLECTION, 2550 The Mall. (96822) Tel. 808/944-8568. Mary Seelye, Reference Libn.
Staff: 2 part time.
Size: 41,563 maps; 450 atlases; 195 aerial photographs; 78 gazetteers.
Annual accessions: 1,650 maps.
Subject specialization: topography.
Depository for: TOPOCOM; USGS (topo); USC&GS.
Serves: University; public.
Interlibrary loan: not available.
Reproduction facilities: photocopy; Xerox.

IDAHO

Boise

155   IDAHO STATE HISTORICAL SOCIETY, 610 North Julia Davis Drive. (83706) Tel. 208/344-5811, ext. 506. Merle Wells, Historian and Archivist.
Staff: 2 part time.
Size: 4,000 maps; 6 atlases; 8 relief models; 60 aerial photographs.
Annual accessions: 200 maps.
Area specializations: Idaho; Pacific Northwest.
Subject specialization: geology.
Special cartographic collection: Idaho township plats from General Land Office surveys.
Serves: public.
Interlibrary loan: available.
Reproduction facilities: photocopy; Xerox; microfilm.

Moscow

156 UNIVERSITY OF IDAHO, LIBRARY, MAP SECTION. (83843) Tel. 208/882-6344. Walter T. McCauley, Social Science Libn.
Staff: 2 part time.
Size: 50,000 maps; 250 atlases; 1 globe.
Annual accessions: 800 maps; 14 atlases.
Area specialization: Pacific Northwest.
Depository for: TOPOCOM; USGS (topo, geol); Canada.
Serves: University; public.
Reproduction facilities: photocopy; Xerox.

Pocatello

157 IDAHO STATE UNIVERSITY, LIBRARY. (83201) Tel. 208/236-3471. T. Min, Social Sciences Libn.
Staff: 1 part time.
Size: 27,778 maps; 70 atlases; 1 globe; 9 relief models; 500 aerial photographs.
Annual accessions: 1,200 maps; 5 atlases.
Area specialization: western United States.
Subject specializations: topography; geology.
Depository for: TOPOCOM; USGS (topo, geol).
Serves: University; public.
Interlibrary loan: not available.
Reproduction facility: Xerox.

Rexburg

158 RICKS COLLEGE, DAVID O. McKAY LIBRARY. (83440) Tel. 208/356-2351. Jerry L. Glenn, Serials and Documents Libn.
Size: 5,641 maps.
Area specializations: Idaho; Mountain States.
Depository for: USGS (topo, geol).
Serves: College; public.
Interlibrary loan: available.
Reproduction facility: Xerox.

ILLINOIS

Carbondale

159 SOUTHERN ILLINOIS UNIVERSITY, SCIENCE LIBRARY, MAP LIBRARY. (62901) Tel. 618/453-2700. Mrs. Jean M. Ray, Acting Map Libn.
Staff: 1 full time; 3 part time.
Size: 115,000 maps; 350 atlases; 4 globes; 100 relief models; 10,000 aerial photographs; 150 gazetteers.
Annual accessions: 5,000 maps; 25 atlases; 20 relief models; 100 aerial photographs; 15 gazetteers.
Area specialization: southern Illinois.
Subject specializations: geology; topography.
Depository for: TOPOCOM; USGS (topo, geol); USC&GS.
Serves: University; public.
Interlibrary loan: available.
Reproduction facility: Xerox.

Charleston

160 EASTERN ILLINOIS UNIVERSITY, BOOTH LIBRARY. (61920) Tel. 217/581-2422. Dr. Leslie T. Andre, Serials and Map Libn.
Staff: 2 part time.
Size: 13,799 maps; 40 atlases; 1 globe; 6 relief models; 3 gazetteers.
Annual accessions: 2,000 maps.
Subject specialization: topography.
Depository for: TOPOCOM, USGS (geol).
Serves: University; public.
Interlibrary loan: not available.
Reproduction facility: Xerox.

Chicago

161 CHICAGO HISTORICAL SOCIETY LIBRARY, North Avenue and Clark Street. (60614) Tel. 312/MI 2-4600. Miss Margaret Scriven, Libn.
Staff: 1 part time.
Size: 10,000 maps; 550 atlases; 5 globes; 63 gazetteers.
Annual accessions: 100 maps; 10 atlases; 10 gazetteers.
Area specializations: Chicago; Illinois; midwestern United States.
Subject specializations: railroads; Indians.
Serves: public.
Interlibrary loan: not available.
Reproduction facilities: photocopy; Xerox; microfilm.

162 CHICAGO MUNICIPAL REFERENCE LIBRARY, Room 1005, City Hall. (60615) Tel.312/744-4992. Joan Sierecki, Head of Technical Processing.
Staff: 2 full time; 1 part time.
Size: 500 maps; 10 atlases; 2 gazetteers.
Annual accessions: 30 maps; 2 atlases.
Area specializations: Chicago; Cook County; Illinois.
Subject specializations: population; transportation.
Serves: public.
Interlibrary loan: not available.
Reproduction facility: Xerox.

163 CHICAGO PUBLIC LIBRARY, HISTORY AND TRAVEL DEPARTMENT, 78 East Washington Street. (60602) Tel. 312/CE 6-8922, ext. 66. Harold Teitelbaum, Chief.
Staff: 1 part time.
Size: 5,000 maps; 325 atlases; 150 gazetteers.
Subject specializations: geography; history.
Serves: public.
Interlibrary loan: available.
Reproduction facility: photocopy.

164 CHICAGO PUBLIC LIBRARY, NATURAL SCIENCES AND USEFUL ARTS DEPARTMENT, 78 East Washington Street. (60602) Tel. 312/CE 6-8922, Ext. 18. Marianne Doherty, Head.
Staff: 2 full time.
Size: 29,680 maps.
Area specialization: Illinois.
Subject specializations: geology; topography; soils.

Depository for: USGS (topo, geol).
Serves: public.
Interlibrary loan: not available.
Reproduction facility: photocopy.

165 CHICAGO PUBLIC LIBRARY, SOCIAL SCIENCES AND BUSINESS DEPARTMENT, 78 East Washington Street. (60602) Tel. 312/CE 6-8922, ext.62. Robert Baumruk, Department Chief.
Staff: 1 part time.
Size: 900 maps; 12 atlases.
Area specialization: Chicago and vicinity.
Serves: public.
Interlibrary loan: available.
Reproduction facility: photocopy.

166 DENOYER-GEPPERT COMPANY, EDITORIAL DEPARTMENT. (60640) Tel. 312/561-9200. Dr. Clarence B. Odell, Vice President and Managing Editor.
Staff: 1 part time.
Size: 4,000 maps; 325 atlases; 30 globes; 15 relief models; 125 gazetteers.
Annual accessions: 200 maps; 10 atlases; 2 globes; 2 relief models; 10 gazetteers.
Serves: employees.
Interlibrary loan: not available.
Reproduction facility: Xerox.

167 NEWBERRY LIBRARY, 60 West Walton Street. (60610) Tel. 312/943-7321. Matt P. Lowman, Curator of Rare Books.
Size: 3,000 maps; 450 atlases; 80 gazetteers.
Annual accessions: 2,100 maps; 10 atlases; 3 gazetteers.
Area specializations: Europe; Western Hemisphere.
Subject specializations: discovery and exploration; geology.
Special cartographic collections: Karpinski Collection of facsimile maps on early American travels; collection of 16th century atlases; European maps; and manuscript maps of North America.
Depository for: USGS (geol).
Serves: public (some restrictions).
Interlibrary loan: not available.
Reproduction facilities: photocopy; Xerox; microfilm.

168 RAND McNALLY, GEOGRAPHIC RESEARCH DEPARTMENT, MAP LIBRARY, P.O. Box 7600. (60680) Tel.312/673-9100, ext. 614. Lee S. Motteler, Libn.
Staff: 2 full time.
Size: 90,000 maps; 1,275 atlases; 5 globes; 25 relief models; 500 gazetteers.
Annual accessions: 3,000 maps; 75 atlases.
Area specializations: United States; Canada.
Subject specializations: topography; place names; transportation; political geography.
Special cartographic collections: books and papers pertaining to cartography.
Serves: employees.
Interlibrary loan: not available.
Reproduction facilities: photocopy; Xerox.
Publications: Map Library Acquisitions Bulletin; A List of Placename Gazetteers of the World.

169 UNIVERSITY OF CHICAGO, LIBRARY, MAP LIBRARY, Rosenwald Hall. (60637) Tel. 312/MI 3-0800, ext. 3448. Agnes Whitmarsh, Map Libn.
Staff: 2 full time.
Size: 211,684 maps; 32 relief models; 9,328 aerial photographs.
Annual accessions: 4,000 maps; 125 aerial photographs.
Area specializations: United States; Canada; USSR; East Asia; southeast Asia; Africa.
Subject specializations: topography; urban geography; transportation; land use; geology; oceanography.
Special cartographic collections: extensive collection of pre-World War II maps of Europe.
Depository for: TOPOCOM; USGS (topo, geol).
Serves: University.
Interlibrary loan: not available.
Reproduction facilities: Xerox; microfilm.

170 UNIVERSITY OF ILLINOIS, CHICAGO CIRCLE CAMPUS, LIBRARY, SPECIAL COLLECTIONS DEPARTMENT*, MAP LIBRARY. (60680).
Depository for: TOPOCOM.

DeKalb

171 NORTHERN ILLINOIS UNIVERSITY, SWEN PARSON LIBRARY, MAP LIBRARY, 227 Davis Hall. (60115) Tel. 815/753-1813. Miss Helen J. Armstrong, Map Libn.
Staff: 2 full time; 4 part time.
Size: 85,000 maps; 253 atlases; 8 globes; 9 relief models; 938 aerial photographs; 85 gazetteers.
Annual accessions: 8,500 maps; 25 atlases; 3 globes; 10 gazetteers.
Area specializations: Canada; Northern Illinois; southeast Asia; India; Moon.
Subject specializations: geology; history; earth sciences; climatology; marketing; economics; topography.
Depository for: TOPOCOM; USGS (topo, geol); Canada; USC&GS.
Serves: University; public.
Interlibrary loan: available.
Reproduction facility: Xerox.
Publication: Monthly Selective Acquisitions List.

Edwardsville

172 SOUTHERN ILLINOIS UNIVERSITY, LOVEJOY LIBRARY, MAP LIBRARY. (62025) Tel. 618/692-2422. Robert L. Koepke, Map Curator.
Staff: 1 part time.
Size: 45,000 maps; 300 atlases; 10 globes; 2,500 aerial photographs.
Annual accessions: 2,500 maps; 15 atlases; 500 aerial photographs.
Area specializations: St.Louis and vicinity; southwestern Illinois; Missouri.
Subject specializations: geology; transportation; mineral resources; topography.
Special cartographic collection: old maps of the Mississippi Valley (originals and copies).
Depository for: TOPOCOM; USGS (topo, geol).
Serves: University; public.
Interlibrary loan: available.
Reproduction facility: Xerox.
Publication: Lovejoy Library Map Lecture Series.

Evanston

173 NORTHWESTERN UNIVERSITY, GRANT MEMORIAL LIBRARY OF GEOLOGY, Locy Hall. (60201) Tel. 312/492-5525. Lillian J. Lee, Geology Libn.

Staff: 3 part time.
Size: not reported.
Annual accessions: 300 maps.
Subject specializations: geology; oceanography; paleontology; geochemistry; geophysics.
Depository for: USGS (geol).
Serves: University.
Interlibrary loan: available.
Reproduction facility: Xerox.

174 NORTHWESTERN UNIVERSITY, MAP LIBRARY. (60201) Tel. 312/492-5207. Mary E. Fortney, Map. Libn.

Staff: 1 full time; 2 part time.
Size: 107,000 maps; 300 atlases; 3 globes; 17 relief models; 1,003 aerial photographs; 67 gazetteers.
Annual accessions: 3,109 maps; 20 atlases; 900 aerial photographs; 5 gazetteers.
Area specialization: Africa.
Depository for: TOPOCOM; USGS (topo); USC&GS (aeronautical and nautical charts).
Serves: University; public.
Interlibrary loan: available.
Reproduction facility: Xerox.

Galesburg

175 KNOX COLLEGE, DEPARTMENT OF GEOLOGY. (61401) Tel. 309/343-1121, ext. 376. Lawrence L. DeMott, Department Head.

Staff: 1 part time.
Size: 8,000 maps.
Annual accessions: 1,200 maps.
Area specialization: United States.
Subject specializations: geology; topography.
Depository for: USGS (topo, geol).
Serves: College; public (by permission).
Interlibrary loan: available.
Reproduction facility: Xerox.

Macomb

176 WESTERN ILLINOIS UNIVERSITY, DEPARTMENT OF GEOGRAPHY, GEOGRAPHY AND MAP LIBRARY. (61455) Tel. 309/899-2989. John V. Bergen, Assistant Professor of Geography and Map Libn.

Staff: 1 full time.
Size: 55,000 maps; 300 atlases; 12 globes; 100 relief models; 1,000 aerial photographs; 40 gazetteers.
Annual accessions: 5,000 maps; 50 atlases.
Area specializations: Illinois; north central United States; Latin America.
Subject specializations: topography; urban geography.
Depository for: TOPOCOM; USGS (topo, geol); Illinois State agencies.
Serves: University; public.

Interlibrary loan: not available.
Reproduction facility: photocopy.

Monmouth

177 MONMOUTH COLLEGE, LIBRARY. (61462) Tel. 309/734-3161, ext. 331. Florence I. Link, Documents and Periodicals Libn.
Staff: 1 full time; 1 part time.
Size: 8,151 maps; 26 atlases; 3 gazetteers.
Subject specializations: geology; topography.
Depository for: USGS (topo, geol).
Serves: College; public.
Interlibrary loan: available.
Reproduction facility: Xerox.

Normal

178 ILLINOIS STATE UNIVERSITY, MILNER LIBRARY, MAP LIBRARY. (61761) Tel. 309/438-8465. William W. Easton, Map Libn.
Staff: 2 full time; 6 part time.
Size: 96,000 maps; 750 atlases; 1 globe; 1 relief model; 36,000 aerial photographs; 200 gazetteers.
Annual accessions: 12,000 maps; 100 atlases; 15,000 aerial photographs; 50 gazetteers.
Area specializations: Illinois; Alaska; United States; Canada; Spain; Japan; Australia; Antarctica.
Subject specializations: topography; oceanography; geology.
Depository for: TOPOCOM; USGS (topo, geol); USC&GS; U.S. Forest Service; other national, state, and city agencies.
Serves: University; public.
Interlibrary loan: available.
Reproduction facility: Xerox.
Publications: accession lists; annual report.

Rock Island.

179 AUGUSTANA COLLEGE, MAP LIBRARY, New Science Building. (61201) Norman Moline, Instructor of Geography.
Staff: 1 part time.
Size: 30,000 maps; 125 atlases; 25 globes; 175 relief models; 4,700 aerial photographs; 50 gazetteers.
Area specializations: Illinois; Scandinavia.
Subject specialization: topography.
Depository for: TOPOCOM; USGS (topo—Illinois).
Serves: College; public (restricted).
Interlibrary loan: available.
Reproduction facility: Xerox.

Skokie

180 INTERNATIONAL MINERALS AND CHEMICALS CORPORATION, EXPLORATION DIVISION LIBRARY, Old Orchard Road. (60076) Tel. 312/Yo 6-3000, ext. 2744. Margaret Slothower.
Staff: 1 part time.

Size: 6,000 maps; 15 atlases;15 relief models; 500 aerial photographs; 20 gazetteers.
Annual accessions: 200 maps.
Area specializations: Idaho; Nevada; Alaska; New Mexico; Florida; Saskatchewan; Mexico; Australia.
Subject specializations: geology; economic geography.
Depository for: USGS (topo, geol); Canada; France (BRGM).
Serves: employees; public (by permission).
Interlibrary loan: available.
Reproduction facility: Xerox.

Springfield

181 ILLINOIS STATE HISTORICAL SOCIETY, LIBRARY. (62706) Tel. 217/425-4836. William K. Alderfer, State Historian.
Staff: 1 part time.
Size: 800 maps; 400 atlases; 35 gazetteers.
Area specializations: Illinois; eastern United States.
Subject specializations: Civil War in Illinois; discovery and exploration of Mississippi Valley.
Serves: public.
Interlibrary loan: not available.
Reproduction facilities: Xerox; microfilm.

182 ILLINOIS STATE LIBRARY, Centennial Building. (62706) Tel. 217/525-2631. Mary MacDonald, Head, Documents Unit.
Size: not reported.
Area specialization: Illinois.
Subject specializations: topography; county atlases and plat books.
Depository for: TOPOCOM; USGS (topo).
Serves: public.
Interlibrary loan: not available.
Reproduction facility: photocopy.

Urbana

183 ILLINOIS STATE GEOLOGICAL SURVEY, GEOLOGICAL RESOURCE RECORDS SECTION, MAP ROOM, 216 Natural Resources Building. (61801) Tel.217/344-1481, ext. 261. Margaret Weatherhead.
Staff: 2 full time.
Size: 14,000 maps; 4,482 aerial photographs.
Area specialization: Illinois.
Subject specialization: geology.
Depository for: USGS (topo, geol).
Serves: employees; public.
Interlibrary loan: not available.

184 UNIVERSITY OF ILLINOIS, GEOLOGY LIBRARY, 223 Natural History Building. (61801) Tel. 217/333-1266. Mrs. Harriet W. Smith, Geology Libn.
Staff: 2 part time.
Size: not reported.
Subject specialization: geology.
Depository for: USGS (geol).
Serves: University; public.
Interlibrary loan: available.

185 UNIVERSITY OF ILLINOIS, ILLINOIS HISTORICAL SURVEY, 1A
Library. (61801) Tel. 217/333-1777. Dr. Robert M. Sutton, Professor of
History and Director.
Staff: 1 full time; 4 part time.
Size: 1,600 maps; 60 atlases; 225 gazetteers.
Area specializations: Illinois; Old Northwest; French Canada.
Subject specializations: history; discovery and exploration; topography.
Special cartographic collections: Manuscript maps of New Harmony and Posey
County, Indiana, catalogued and described by Arthur E. Bestor, Jr.; Karpinski
Collection.
Serves: University; public.
Interlibrary loan: not available.
Reproduction facilities: Xerox; microfilm.
Publications: numerous published guides and checklists describing manuscript
materials in the Illinois Historical Survey.

186 UNIVERSITY OF ILLINOIS, MAP AND GEOGRAPHY LIBRARY.
(61801) Tel. 217/333-0827. Robert C. White, Map and Geography Libn.
Staff: 2 full time; 4 part time.
Size: 249,800 maps; 3,700 atlases; 7 globes; 30 relief models; 85,600 aerial
photographs; 700 gazetteers.
Annual accessions: 6,000 maps; 35 atlases; 400 aerial photographs.
Area specializations: Illinois; United States; Latin America; western and central
Europe.
Subject specializations: agriculture; city planning; climatology; geology;
topography.
Special cartographic collections: cartographic techniques; historical cartography.
Depository for: TOPOCOM; USGS (topo, geol); USC&GS; U.S. Lake Survey.
Serves: University; public.
Interlibrary loan: available.
Reproduction facilities: photocopy; Xerox; microfilm.
Publications: New Acquisitions (bi-monthly); *Maps and Books in the Library*
(annual).

Wheaton

187 WHEATON COLLEGE, DEPARTMENT OF POLITICAL SCIENCE.*
(60188) Frank Bellinger.
Depository for: TOPOCOM.

INDIANA

Bloomington

188 INDIANA UNIVERSITY, DEPARTMENT OF GEOGRAPHY, MAP
LIBRARY. (47401) Tel. 812/337-8651. Robert D. Plank, Map Libn.
Staff: 1 full time; 3 part time.
Size: 125,000 maps; 500 atlases; 300 relief models; 7,500 aerial photographs; 200
gazetteers.
Annual accessions: 5,000 maps; 100 atlases; 25 gazetteers.
Area specialization: Indiana.
Subject specializations: geography; topography.
Depository for: TOPOCOM; U.S. Lake Survey.

Serves: University; public.
Interlibrary loan: available.
Reproduction facility: photocopy.
Publication: Map Library Accession List (monthly).

189 INDIANA UNIVERSTIY, DEPARTMENT OF GEOLOGY AND INDI-
ANA GEOLOGICAL SURVEY, GEOLOGY LIBRARY, 1005 East 10th
Street. (47401) Tel. 812/337-7170. Miss Ellen L. Freeman, Libn.
Staff: 1 part time.
Size: 85,000 maps; 35 atlases; 1 globe; 19 relief models; 3 gazetteers.
Annual accessions: 5,000 maps.
Area specializations: Indiana; Montana; United States.
Subject specializations: geology; mineral resources; oil and gas.
Depository for: USGS (topo, geol); exchanges with over 100 governmental agencies
worldwide.
Serves: University; public.
Reproduction facility: Xerox.

Fort Wayne

190 FORT WAYNE AND ALLEN COUNTY PUBLIC LIBRARY, 900
Webster Street. (46802) Tel. 219/742-7241, ext. 247. William H. Crane,
Documents Libn.
Staff: 3 part time.
Size: 2,000 maps; 50 atlases; 2 globes; 1 relief model; 5 gazetteers.
Area specializations: Indiana; United States.
Subject specialization: topography.
Serves: public.
Interlibrary loan: not available.
Reproduction facility: photocopy.

Greencastle

191 DEPAUW UNIVERSITY, ROY O. WEST LIBRARY. (46135) Tel. 317/
653-9721, ext. 354. Mrs. Emily Alward, Documents Libn.
Staff: 1 part time.
Size: 30,000 maps; 30 atlases; 1 globe; 110 gazetteers.
Annual accessions: 2,100 maps; 2 atlases; 10 gazetteers.
Subject specializations: topography; geology.
Depository for: USGS (topo, geol).
Serves: University; public.
Interlibrary loan: available (restricted).
Reproduction facility: Xerox.

Hanover

192 HANOVER COLLEGE, DEPARTMENT OF GEOLOGY. (47243) Tel.
812/866-2151, ext. 307. Clifford Adams, Department Chairman.
Staff: 1 part time.
Size: 5,000 maps; 12 globes; 25 relief models; 100 aerial photographs.
Annual accessions: 500 maps.
Subject specializations: geology; topography.
Depository for: USGS (topo, geol).
Serves: College; public.

Interlibrary loan: not available.
Reproduction facility: Xerox.

Indianapolis

193   INDIANA HISTORICAL SOCIETY, LIBRARY, Room 206, 140 North Senate Avenue. (46204) Tel. 317/633-4976. Caroline Dunn, Libn.
Size: 500 maps; 100 atlases; 20 gazetteers.
Annual accessions: 10 maps; 2 atlases.
Area specializations: Indiana; Ohio Valley; Old Northwest Territory.
Subject specialization: local history.
Special cartographic collection: Karpinski Collection (photocopies).
Serves: public.
Interlibrary loan: not available.
Reproduction facilities: photocopy; Xerox; microfilm.

194   INDIANAPOLIS–MARION COUNTY PUBLIC LIBRARY, 40 East St. Clair Street. (46204) Tel. 317/638-4552.
Size: 1,400 maps; 130 atlases; 1 globe; 30 aerial photographs; 3 gazetteers.
Serves: public.
Interlibrary loan: available.
Reproduction facility: Xerox.

Muncie

195   BALL STATE UNIVERSITY, LIBRARY, ~~TEACHING MATERIALS SERVICE.~~ (47306) Tel. ~~317/285-5628.~~ Vera M. McCoskey, Libn.
Size: 813 maps (TOPOCOM maps not in total); 6 globes.
Subject specializations: topography.
Depository for: TOPOCOM.
Serves: University.
Interlibrary loan: not available.

[handwritten: Map Collection]
[handwritten: 317-285-4077]

Notre Dame

196   UNIVERSITY OF NOTRE DAME, GEOLOGY LIBRARY. (46556) Tel. 219/283-6686. R. C. Gutschick, Department Chairman.
Staff: 1 part time.
Size: 10,000 maps; 5 atlases; 1 globe; 100 relief models; 200 aerial photographs.
Annual accessions: 500 maps; 15 relief models; 20 aerial photographs.
Area specialization: United States.
Subject specializations: geology; topography.
Depository for: USGS (topo, geol); Canada.
Serves: University; public.
Interlibrary loan: available.
Reproduction facilities: photocopy; Xerox; microfilm.

197   UNIVERSITY OF NOTRE DAME, MEMORIAL LIBRARY. (46556) Tel. 219/283-6134.
Size: 40,000 maps; 60 atlases; 1 globe; 10 gazetteers.
Depository for: TOPOCOM.
Serves: University; public.
Interlibrary loan: not available.
Reproduction facilities: Xerox; microfilm.

Rensselaer

198 SAINT JOSEPH'S COLLEGE, DEPARTMENT OF GEOLOGY. (47978) Tel. 219/866-5649. Michael E. Davis, Associate Professor of Geology.
Staff: 2 part time.
Size: 40,000 maps; 10 atlases; 2 globes; 300 aerial photographs.
Annual accessions: 2,000 maps; 2 atlases; 20 aerial photographs.
Subject specializations: geology; topography; river surveys.
Depository for: USGS (topo, geol).
Serves: College; public.
Reproduction facility: Xerox.

Terre Haute

199 HISTORICAL MUSEUM OF THE WABASH VALLEY, 1411 South Sixth Street. (47802) Tel. 812/235-9717. Mrs. Dorothy J. Clark, Secretary and Curator.
Size: 100 maps; 10 atlases; 1 relief model.
Area specializations: Wabash Valley; Vigo County; Terre Haute.
Subject specializations: local history; genealogy.
Special cartographic collection: early Terre Haute plat maps.
Serves: public.
Interlibrary loan: not available.
Reproduction facilities: photocopy; Xerox; microfilm.

200 INDIANA STATE UNIVERSITY, DEPARTMENT OF GEOGRAPHY AND GEOLOGY, MAP LIBRARY. (47809) Tel. 812/232-6311. Dr. Benjamin Moulton, Department Chairman.
Staff: 3 part time.
Size: 120,000 maps; 6 relief models; 2,000 aerial photographs.
Annual accessions: 10,000 maps; 2 relief models; 1,000 aerial photographs.
Area specialization: North America.
Subject specializations: geology; topography.
Depository for: TOPOCOM; USGS (topo, geol).
Serves: University; public.
Interlibrary loan: not available.
Reproduction facilities: photocopy; Xerox.

Valparaiso

201 VALPARAISO UNIVERSITY, DEPARTMENT OF GEOGRAPHY, MAP LIBRARY. (46383) Tel. 219/462-5111, ext. 275. Elmer B. Hess, Assistant Professor of Geography.
Staff: 1 part time.
Size: 25,000 maps; 22 atlases; 10 globes; 8 relief models.
Annual accessions: 1,000 maps.
Subject specialization: topography.
Depository for: TOPOCOM; USGS (topo).
Serves: University.
Interlibrary loan: not available.
Reproduction facility: Xerox.

West Lafayette

202 PURDUE UNIVERSITY, LIBRARY, MAP COLLECTION, Memorial Center. (47907) Tel. 317/749-2557. Mrs. Anne Black, Reference Assistant.

Staff: 1 full time; 1 part time.
Size: 69,000 maps; 275 atlases; 15 relief models; 200 gazetteers.
Annual accessions: 2,000 maps; 25 atlases; 25 gazetteers.
Area specialization: Indiana.
Subject specializations: topography; geology; geography.
Special cartographic collections: Theatrum Orbis Terrarum, atlases in facsimile, 1477–1689; *Portugaliae Monumenta Cartographica,* history of Portuguese cartography.
Depository for: TOPOCOM; USGS (topo, geol).
Serves: University; public.
Interlibrary loan: available.
Reproduction facilities: photocopy; Xerox.

IOWA

Cedar Rapids

203 CEDAR RAPIDS PUBLIC LIBRARY, 428 3rd Avenue S.E. (52401) Tel. 319/366-1561. Ruth Richardson, Head of Adult Services.
Size: 1,200 maps; 70 atlases; 1 globe; 3 gazetteers.
Serves: public.
Interlibrary loan: available.
Reproduction facility: Dennison copier.

Des Moines

204 IOWA (STATE) DEPARTMENT OF HISTORY AND ARCHIVES, LIBRARY. East 12th and Grand Avenue. (50319) Lida L. Greene, Libn.
Size: 700 maps; 350 atlases; 15 gazetteers.
Area specializations: Iowa; Midwestern United States.
Subject specialization: history.
Serves: public.
Interlibrary loan: not available.
Reproduction facility: microfilm.

Dubuque

205 CARNEGIE-STOUT PUBLIC LIBRARY, 11th and Bluff Streets. (52001) Tel. 319/583-9197. Mrs. Maxine Baer.
Staff: 1 part time.
Size: 443 maps.
Area specializations: Iowa; southwestern Wisconsin; northwestern Illinois.
Subject specialization: topography.
Depository for: USGS (topo—midwestern states).
Serves: public.
Interlibrary loan: not available.
Reproduction facility: photocopy.

Harlan

206 R. C. BOOTH ENTERPRISES. (51537) Tel. 712/755-1425. Maxine Thielen.
Size: 300 maps; 200 atlases.

Area specializations: Iowa; midwestern United States.
Special cartographic collections: farm ownership atlases; school district maps; city plat maps; county rural resident maps.
Serves: public.
Interlibrary loan: not available.
Reproduction facility: Ozalid.

Iowa City

207 UNIVERSITY OF IOWA, GEOLOGY LIBRARY. (52240) Tel. 319/353-4225. Miss Vera J. Bacon, Libn.
Staff: 1 full time.
Size: 35,000 maps; 4 atlases; 1 gazetteer.
Subject specialization: geology.
Depository for: USGS (topo, geol); Canada.
Serves: University; public.
Interlibrary loan: not available.
Reproduction facilities: Xerox; microfilm.

208 UNIVERSITY OF IOWA, LIBRARY, MAP COLLECTION. (52240) Tel. 319/353-4482. Albert Perdue, Libn. 319/353-4467
Staff: 2 full time.   WATS 167-3-4467   Richard Green, Libr.
Size: 40,697 maps; 1,138 atlases and gazetteers; 9 relief models; 50,161 aerial photographs.
Annual accessions: 7,263 maps; 441 atlases; 3,430 aerial photographs.
Area specializations: Iowa; midwestern United States.
Special cartographic collections: captured German and Japanese military maps.
Depository for: TOPOCOM.   8 - 5 m- F
Serves: University; public.
Interlibrary loan: available.   Sat.
Reproduction facility: Xerox.

Waterloo

209 MUSEUM OF HISTORY AND SCIENCE, REFERENCE LIBRARY, 503 South Street. (50701) Tel. 319/234-6357. Mrs. Genevieve Woodbridge, Director.
Staff: 1 full time.
Size: 201 maps; 37 atlases; 2 globes; 21 gazetteers.
Area specializations: Black Hawk County; Iowa.
Subject specializations: history; Indian culture.
Special cartographic collection: Old maps of midwestern United States.
Serves: public.
Interlibrary loan: not available.

KANSAS

Lawrence

210 UNIVERSITY OF KANSAS, MAP LIBRARY, Room 110, Kenneth Spencer Research Library. (66044) Tel. 913/864-2700. Mrs. Jennie Dienes, Library Assistant.
Staff: 1 full time; 2 part time.
Size: 120,000 maps; 300 atlases; 200 aerial photographs; 200 gazetteers.
Annual accessions: 3,000 maps; 25 atlases; 25 gazetteers.
Area specialization: comprehensive.

Subject specializations: geology; historical cartography; topography.
Special cartographic collection: maps illustrating the development of cartography of the Americas prior to 1800.
Depository for: TOPOCOM; USGS (topo, geol).
Serves: University; public.
Interlibrary loan: available (restricted).
Reproduction facility: photocopy.

Topeka

211 KANSAS STATE HISTORICAL SOCIETY, Memorial Building, 120 West 10th Street. (66612) Tel. 913/233-8951, ext. 23 or 24. Robert W. Richmond, State Archivist.
Staff: 5 full time.
Size: 6,441 maps and atlases.
Annual accessions: 91 maps and atlases.
Area specializations: Kansas; western United States.
Subject specialization: geology.
Depository for: USGS (geol); USC&GS (aeronautical charts).
Serves: public.
Interlibrary loan: not available.
Reproduction facilities: photocopy (available commercially); Xerox; microfilm.

Wichita

212 WICHITA PUBLIC LIBRARY, 223 South Main Street. (67202) Tel. 316/ AM 5-5281. Ford A. Rockwell, Libn.
Size: 2,300 maps.
Area specialization: Kansas.
Subject specializations: geography; geodesy.
Serves: public.
Interlibrary loan: available.
Reproduction facility: photocopy.

KENTUCKY

Berea

213 BEREA COLLEGE, DEPARTMENT OF GEOLOGY AND GEOGRAPHY. (40403) Tel. 606/986-9927. Zelek L. Lipchinsky, Department Chairman.
Staff: 1 part time.
Size: 6,000 maps; 5 atlases; 3 globes; 20 relief models.
Annual accessions: 500 maps; 5 relief models.
Area specializations: Kentucky; Appalachian Mountains.
Subject specializations: geology; topography.
Depository for: USGS (topo, geol).
Serves: College; public.
Interlibrary loan: available.
Reproduction facilities: photocopy; Xerox.

Frankfort

214 KENTUCKY (STATE) DEPARTMENT OF COMMERCE, Bush Building. (40601) Tel. 502/564-4715. Victor Banta.

Staff: 3 full time.
Size: 158,152 maps; 3,000 atlases; 68,034 aerial photographs.
Annual accessions: 40 maps; 9 atlases; 200 aerial photographs.
Subject specializations: mineral resources; industrial development; topography.
Depository for: USGS (topo, geol).
Serves: public.
Interlibrary loan: not available.
Reproduction facility: Xerox.

Lexington

215 UNIVERSTIY OF KENTUCKY, GEOLOGY LIBRARY. (40506) Tel. 606/258-9000, ext. 2138. Mrs. Vivian S. Hall, Geology Libn.
Staff: 1 full time; 7 part time.
Size: 44,000 maps; 200 atlases; 1 globe.
Subject specializations: topography; geology.
Depository for: USGS (topo, geol); Canada.
Serves: University; public.
Interlibrary loan: not available.
Reproduction facility: Xerox.

216 UNIVERSITY OF KENTUCKY, KING LIBRARY, SPECIAL COLLECTIONS DEPARTMENT*. (40506) Tel. 606/258-9000, ext. 2821.
Depository for: TOPOCOM.

LOUISIANA

Baton Rouge

217 LOUISIANA STATE LIBRARY, LOUISIANA DEPARTMENT, P.O. Box 131. (70821) Tel. 504/389-6120. Mrs. Edith Atkinson, Libn.
Staff: 1 part time.
Size: 1,622 maps; 30 atlases.
Area specializations: Louisiana; lower Mississippi Valley; Mississippi River; Gulf of Mexico.
Serves: public.
Interlibrary loan: available.
Reproduction facilities: photocopy; Xerox.

218 LOUISIANA STATE UNIVERSITY, DEPARTMENT OF ARCHIVES AND MANUSCRIPTS. (70803) Tel. 504/388-2240. V. L. Bedsole, Department Head.
Size: 1,200 maps.
Area specializations: Louisiana; lower Mississippi Valley.
Subject specializations: local history; transportation; land ownership.
Serves: University; public.
Interlibrary loan: not available.

219 LOUISIANA STATE UNIVERSITY, SCHOOL OF GEOLOGY, MAP ROOM. (70803) Tel. 504/388-6561. Dr. Milton B. Newton, Jr., Curator.
Staff: 1 full time; 5 part time.
Size: 180,000 maps; 50 atlases; 4 globes; 10 relief models; 60,000 aerial photographs; 50 gazetteers.
Annual accessions: 5,000 maps; 5 atlases.

Area specializations: Louisiana; southeastern United States; Central America.
Subject specializations: geology; physical geography.
Depository for: TOPOCOM; USGS (topo, geol); Canada; USC&GS; Louisiana Attorney General.
Serves: University; public.
Interlibrary loan: available (restricted).
Reproduction facility: photocopy.

New Orleans

220 NEW ORLEANS PUBLIC LIBRARY, LOUISIANA DIVISION, 219 Loyola Avenue. (70140) Tel. 504/523-4602. Collin B. Hamer, Jr., Division Head.
Size: 700 maps; 10 atlases; 7,000 aerial photographs.
Area specializations: Louisiana; New Orleans.
Subject specializations: local history.
Depository for: USGS (topo, geol).
Serves: public.
Interlibrary loan: not available.
Reproduction facilities: commercial facilities available locally.

221 TULANE UNIVERSITY, LATIN AMERICAN LIBRARY. (70118) Tel. 504/865-7711, ext. 7628. Marjorie LeDoux, Libn.
Staff: 1 full time.
Size: 1,500 maps; 90 atlases.
Annual accessions: 5 maps; 2 atlases.
Area specializations: Central America; South America.
Subject specializations: archaeology; history.
Serves: University; public.
Interlibrary loan: not available.
Reproduction facilities: photocopy; Xerox; microfilm.

MAINE

Bangor

222 BANGOR PUBLIC LIBRARY, 145 Harlow Street. (04401) Tel. 207/945-5000. Olive M. Smythe, Reference Libn.
Staff: 1 part time.
Size: 23,000 maps; 431 atlases; 4 globes; 40 aerial photographs; 18 gazetteers.
Area specialization: Maine.
Subject specialization: topography.
Depository for: USGS (topo—selective).
Serves: public.
Interlibrary loan: not available.
Reproduction facility: Xerox.

Brunswick

223 BOWDOIN COLLEGE, LIBRARY. (04011) Tel. 207/725-8731, ext. 288. Robert L. Volz, Special Collections Libn.
Staff: 1 part time.
Size: 40,000 maps; 100 atlases.

Area specialization: Maine.
Depository for: TOPOCOM; USGS (topo); Geological Survey of Alabama; Canada (GSC).
Serves: College; public.
Interlibrary loan: not available.
Reproduction facility: Xerox.

Lewiston

224 BATES COLLEGE, GEOLOGY DEPARTMENT. (04240) Tel. 207/784-9159. Dr. Roy L. Farnsworth, Department Chairman.
Size: not reported.
Subject specialization: topography.
Depository for: USGS (topo).
Serves: College; public.

Orono

225 UNIVERSITY OF MAINE, RAYMOND H. FOGLER LIBRARY, TRI-STATE DOCUMENT DEPOSITORY. (04473) Tel. 207/866-7178. Mrs. Barbara MacCampbell, Documents Libn.
Staff: 1 full time.
Size: not reported.
Depository for: TOPOCOM; USGS (topo, geol).
Serves: University; public.
Interlibrary loan: available.
Reproduction facilities: Xerox; microfilm.

Portland

226 MAINE HISTORICAL SOCIETY, 485 Congress Street. (04111) Tel. 207/774-9351. John Janitz, Manuscript Libn.
Size: Several thousand maps; 70 gazetteers.
Area specialization: Maine.
Subject specializations: land litigation maps; Civil War maps; 19th century sea charts.
Special cartographic collections: Pejepscot (VIII) papers (Plymouth Company Records); Northeastern Boundary Commission official atlas, 1815–1840; J. F. W. Des Barres' *The Atlantic Neptune.*
Serves: public.
Interlibrary loan: not available.
Reproduction facility: photocopy.
Publication: Maine Historical Society (brochure).

227 PORTLAND PUBLIC LIBRARY, REFERENCE DEPARTMENT, 619 Congress Street. (04101) Tel. 207/772-8030. Eugenia M. Southard, Reference Libn.
Staff: 2 full time; 1 part time.
Size: 16,000 maps; 82 atlases; 1 globe; 19 gazetteers.
Annual accessions: 2,400 maps; 10 atlases; 2 gazetteers.
Area specializations: Maine; United States.
Subject specializations: geology; topography.
Special cartographic collections: 19th century county maps of Maine.
Depository for: USGS (topo).
Serves: public.

Interlibrary loan: not available.
Reproduction facility: Xerox.

Waterville

228   COLBY COLLEGE, GEOLOGY DEPARTMENT, MAP COLLECTION.
(04901) Tel. 207/873-1131, ext.241. Harold R. Pestana, Assistant Professor.
Staff: 1 part time.
Size: 42,000 maps.
Annual accessions: 1,200 maps.
Area specialization: United States.
Subject specialization: geology.
Depository for: USGS (topo).
Serves: College; public.

MARYLAND

Baltimore

229   ENOCH PRATT FREE LIBRARY, DOCUMENTS DIVISION*, 400
Cathedral Street. (21201) Tel. 301/685-6700.
Depository for: TOPOCOM.

230   ENOCH PRATT FREE LIBRARY, GEORGE PEABODY BRANCH,
17th East Mt. Venon Place. (21202) Tel. 301/837-9100, ext. 334 or 335.
Clayton E. Rhodes, Acting Librarian.
Size: not reported.
Area specializations: Baltimore; Maryland; United States; western Europe.
Subject specializations: local history; early maps of Maryland and Baltimore;
16th–19th century atlases.
Serves: public.
Interlibrary loan: available (restricted).
Reproduction facilities: Xerox; microfilm.

231   MARYLAND HISTORICAL SOCIETY, 201 West Monument Street.
(21201) Tel. 301/685-3750, ext. 72. Mrs. Robert H. McCauley, Jr., Curator
of Graphics.
Staff: 1 full time.
Size: 1,600 maps; 27 atlases; 5 gazetteers.
Area specialization: Maryland.
Subject specializations: city and county maps; history.
Serves: public.
Reproduction facilities: photocopy; Xerox.
Publication: accessions are published in *Maryland History Notes* (quarterly).

College Park

232   UNIVERSITY OF MARYLAND, DEPARTMENT OF GEOGRAPHY,
GEOGRAPHY REFERENCE LIBRARY. (20740) Tel. 301/454-2242.
William A. Dando.
Staff: 2 full time; 2 part time.
Size: 85,000 maps; 600 atlases; 10 globes; 100 relief models; 17,000 aerial
photographs; 50 gazetteers.
Annual accessions: 1,000 maps; 50 atlases; 10 gazetteers.

Area specializations: Maryland; Africa; USSR.
Subject specializations: geomorphology; climatology; physical geography.
Serves: University; public.
Interlibrary loan: not available.
Publications: accessions lists.

233 UNIVERSITY OF MARYLAND, McKELDIN LIBRARY, REFERENCE DEPARTMENT, MAP SECTION*. (20742) Tel. 301/454-3011.
Depository for: TOPOCOM.

Frostburg

234 FROSTBURG STATE COLLEGE, JEROME FRAMPTOM LIBRARY. (21532) Tel. 301/689-6621, ext. 222. Ann Comer, Archivist.
Size: 3,000 maps.
Area specializations: Maryland; United States.
Subject specialization: topography.
Depository for: USGS (topo).
Serves: College; public.
Interlibrary loan: not available.
Reproduction facility: Xerox.

Rockville

235 U.S. COAST AND GEODETIC SURVEY, MAP SERVICES BRANCH. (20852) Tel. 301/496-8031. Jack Campbell, Chief, Map Services Branch.
Staff: 4 full time.
Size: *350,000 maps; 250 atlases; several thousand aerial photographs.
Serves: employees.
Interlibrary loan: not available.
Reproduction facility: photocopy.

Silver Spring

236 U.S. ENVIRONMENTAL SCIENCE SERVICES ADMINISTRATION, ATMOSPHERIC SCIENCES LIBRARY. (20910) Tel. 301/495-2401. Marjorie Clark, Chief, Reference and Circulation Unit.
Area specialization: worldwide.
Subject specializations: meteorology; climatology; hydrology.
Special cartographic collection: extensive collection of daily weather maps from most of the countries throughout the world.
Serves: public.
Interlibrary loan: available.

MASSACHUSETTS

Amherst

237 AMHERST COLLEGE, LIBRARY. (01002) Tel. 413/542-2373 or 2319. Floyd S. Merritt, Reference Libn.
Staff: 2 part time.
Size: over 24,000 maps; 175 gazetteers.
Area specialization: New England.
Subject specializations: geology; topography.

Depository for: TOPOCOM; USGS (topo, geol).
Serves: College; registered readers.
Interlibrary loan: not available.
Reproduction facilities: photocopy; Xerox.

238 UNIVERSITY OF MASSACHUSETTS, GOODELL LIBRARY*. (01003)
Tel. 617/545-2233.
Depository for: TOPOCOM.

Boston

239 BOSTON ATHENAEUM, 10½ Beacon Street. (02108) Tel. 617/CA 7-0270.
Peter R. Haack, Assistant Libn.
Size: 4,000 maps; 600 atlases; 3 globes. (Data from *Directory of Map Collections*
. . ., 1954)
Depository for: USGS (topo).
Serves: public.
Reproduction facilities: photocopy; microfilm.

240 BOSTON PUBLIC LIBRARY, Copley Square. (02117) Tel. 617/536-5400.
Martin F. Waters, Curator of Geography and Maps.
Size: 320,000 maps; 2,000 atlases; 800 gazetteers.
Area specializations: Boston; New England; United States; Great Britain; Canada.
Subject specializations: topography; history.
Special cartographic collection: 16th and 17th century atlases and maps.
Depository for: TOPOCOM; USGS (topo).
Serves: public.
Interlibrary loan: not available.
Reproduction facilities: photocopy; Xerox; microfilm.

241 BOSTON UNIVERSITY, MUGAR MEMORIAL LIBRARY, MAP
ROOM, 771 Commonwealth Avenue. (02135) Tel. 617/353-3717. Mrs.
Daniel Friedenson, General Libn.
Staff: 1 full time; 1 part time.
Size: 1,500 maps; 200 atlases; 1 globe; 2 gazetteers.
Area specialization: Africa.
Subject specialization: history.
Serves: University; public.
Interlibrary loan: not available.
Reproduction facilities: photocopy; Xerox.

242 BOSTONIAN SOCIETY, Old State House, 206 Washington Street. (02109)
Tel. 617/523-7033. Mrs. Ropes Cabot, Curator.
Staff: 1 part time.
Size: 500 maps; 25 atlases; 4 aerial photographs.
Annual accessions: 5 maps.
Area specialization: Boston.
Serves: public.
Interlibrary loan: not available.
Reproduction facilities: photocopy; Xerox; microfilm.

243 CHRISTIAN SCIENCE MONITOR, LIBRARY, One Norway Street.
(02115) Tel. 617/262-2300, ext. 2681. Chester W. Sanger, Library Manager.
Size: 18,000 maps; 40 atlases. (Data from *Directory of Map Collections* . . ., 1954)
Serves: employees.

244   INSURANCE LIBRARY ASSOCIATION, 89 Broad Street. (02110) Tel. 617/426-3466. Priscilla Biondi, Libn.

Size: 521 maps.
Special cartographic collection: Sanborn fire insurance maps for most New England towns and cities excluding Boston.
Serves: members.
Interlibrary loan: not available.

245   MASSACHUSETTS HISTORICAL SOCIETY, 1154 Boylston Street. (02215) Tel. 617/KE 6-1608. John D. Cushing, Libn.

Size: 3,000 maps; 500 atlases.
Area specializations: Massachusetts; New England.
Subject specialization: local history.
Serves: public.
Interlibrary loan: not available.
Reproduction facility: Xerox.

246   MASSACHUSETTS STATE LIBRARY, 341 State House. (02114) Tel. 617/ 727-2590. Alan Fox, Assistant Libn.

Size: 21,800 maps; 400 atlases; 40 gazetteers.
Area specialization: New England.
Subject specialization: local history.
Depository for: State of Massachusetts.
Serves: public.
Interlibrary loan: not available.
Reproduction facilities: photocopy; Xerox.

247   SOCIETY FOR THE PRESERVATION OF NEW ENGLAND AN-TIQUITIES, 141 Cambridge Street. (02114) Tel. 617/227-3960. Mrs. Robin D. Whitney, Assistant Libn.

Staff: 1 part time.
Size: 100 maps; 20 atlases.
Area specialization: New England.
Special cartographic collection: old county maps and atlases.
Interlibrary loan: not available.
Reproduction facility: photocopy.

Cambridge

248   HARVARD COLLEGE LIBRARY, THE WINSOR MEMORIAL MAP ROOM. (02138) Tel. 617/868-7600, ext. 2417. Dr. Frank E. Trout, Curator of Maps.

Staff: 3 full time; 1 part time.
Size: 150,000 maps; 800 wall maps; 1,700 atlases; 7 globes; 25 relief models; 250 aerial photographs. (Data from *Directory of Map Collections* . . ., 1954)
Area specializations: United States; Europe; USSR.
Subject specialization: topography.
Depository for: TOPOCOM; USGS (topo).
Serves: College.
Interlibrary loan: not available.
Reproduction facilities: photocopy; Xerox; microfilm.

249   HARVARD UNIVERSITY, DEPARTMENT OF GEOLOGICAL SCIEN-CES, MAP ROOM, 24 Oxford Street. (02138) Tel. 617/868-7600, ext. 2029. Dr. John Haller, Associate Professor, Department of Geological Sciences.

Staff: 1 part time.
Size: not reported.
Area specializations: North America; Europe; Asia.
Subject specialization: geology.
Depository for: USGS (geol).
Serves: University; others by special permission.
Interlibrary loan: not available.
Reproduction facility: Xerox.

250 MASSACHUSETTS INSTITUTE OF TECHNOLOGY, LINDGREN LIBRARY, Room 54-200. (02139) Tel. 617/864-6900, ext. 5679. Mrs. Suanne Muehlner, Acting Lindgren Libn.
Size: 4,500 maps; 140 atlases; 2 globes; 1 gazetteer.
Annual accessions: 150 maps.
Area specialization: United States.
Subject specializations: geology; geophysics.
Depository for: USGS (geol).
Serves: Institute.
Reproduction facilities: photocopy; Xerox; microfilm.

251 MASSACHUSETTS INSTITUTE OF TECHNOLOGY, ROTCH LIBRARY OF ARCHITECTURE AND PLANNING, Room 7-238. (02139) Tel. 617/864-6900, ext. 7053. Patricia Pier, Reference Libn.
Size: 600 maps and aerial photographs; 66 atlases; 1 globe; 3 gazetteers.
Annual accessions: 10 maps; 3 atlases.
Area specializations: Boston; Massachusetts.
Special cartographic collection: Sanborn fire insurance atlases for Greater Boston.
Serves: Institute; public.
Interlibrary loan: not available.

252 MASSACHUSETTS INSTITUTE OF TECHNOLOGY, SCIENCE LIBRARY, BOSTON STEIN CLUB MAP ROOM, Room 14S-100. (02139) Tel. 617/864-6900, ext. 5685. Mrs. Ching-chih Chen, Assistant Science Libn.
Size: 52,000 maps; 50 atlases; 20 globes; 24 gazetteers.
Annual accessions: 2,000 maps.
Subject specialization: topography.
Depository for: TOPOCOM; USGS (topo).
Serves: Institute.
Reproduction facilities: photocopy; Xerox; microfilm.

Medford

253 TUFTS UNIVERSITY. (02155) Tel. 617/628-5000. James D. Hume, Associate Professor of Geology.
Staff: 1 part time.
Size: maps not reported; 5 atlases; 2 globes; 200 relief models; 1,000 aerial photographs.
Annual accessions: 5 relief models; 200 aerial photographs.
Subject specializations: geology; topography; petrology.
Depository for: USGS (topo, geol).
Serves: University; public.
Reproduction facility: Xerox.

Northampton

254 SMITH COLLEGE, DEPARTMENT OF GEOLOGY, MAP LIBRARY. (01060) Richard K. Bambach, Assistant Professor of Geology.

Staff: 1 part time.
Size: 50,000 maps; 80 gazetteers.
Annual accessions: 300 maps.
Area specialization: United States.
Subject specializations: topography; geology.
Depository for: TOPOCOM; USGS (topo, geol).
Serves: College.
Interlibrary loan: not available.

Salem

255 ESSEX INSTITUTE, 132 Essex Street. (01970) Tel. 617/744-3390. Mrs. Charles A. Potter, Libn.
Size: not reported.
Area specialization: Essex County.
Subject specialization: civil history.
Serves: public.
Interlibrary loan: available (restricted).
Reproduction facility: Xerox.

South Hadley

256 MOUNT HOLYOKE COLLEGE, DEPARTMENT OF GEOGRAPHY AND GEOLOGY. (01075) Tel. 413/536-4000, ext 468, 334 or 324.
Staff: 1 full time.
Size: 6,000 maps; 100 atlases; 4 globes; 25 relief models; 300 aerial photographs; 52 gazetteers.
Area specializations: Latin America; Great Britain.
Subject specialization: regional planning.
Depository for: USGS (topo, geol).
Serves: College; public.
Interlibrary loan: available.
Reproduction facility: Tecnifax photo modifier.

Wellesley

257 WELLESLEY COLLEGE, DEPARTMENT OF GEOLOGY. (02181) Tel. 617/253-0320, ext. 378. Jerome Regnier.
Size: maps not reported; 140 atlases; 3 globes; 25 relief models.
Area specialization: United States.
Depository for: TOPOCOM; USGS (topo, geol).
Serves: College; public.
Interlibrary loan: not available.

Williamstown

258 WILLIAMS COLLEGE, DEPARTMENT OF GEOLOGY. (01267) Tel. 413/458-7131, ext. 249.
Staff: 1 part time.
Size: 37,000 maps; 6 atlases; 2 globes; 15 relief models; 1 gazetteer.
Subject specializations: geology; topography.
Depository for: USGS (topo, geol); Massachusetts State Geological Survey.
Serves: College; public.
Interlibrary loan: available.

Woods Hole

259 WOODS HOLE OCEANOGRAPHIC INSTITUTION, CHART AND MAP REFERENCE LIBRARY. (02543) Tel. 617/548-1400, ext. 386 or 387. William M. Dunkle, Research Associate.
Staff: 2 full time; 1 part time.
Size: 500 maps; 300 atlases; 6,080 charts; 50 relief models.
Annual accessions: 75 maps; 40 atlases; 500 charts; 10 relief models.
Area specialization: world oceans.
Subject specializations: geology; bathymetry; hydrography; oceanography; topography.
Depository for: USGS (topo, geol-selective); USC&GS; NOC; Canada; Great Britain; France.
Serves: Institution; public.
Interlibrary loan: available.
Reproduction facilities: photocopy; Xerox; microfilm.

Worcester

260 AMERICAN ANTIQUARIAN SOCIETY, 185 Salisbury Street. (01609) Tel. 617/755-5221. Mrs. Louise S. Marshall, Curator of Maps and Prints.
Staff: 1 full time.
Size: 9,800 maps; 560 atlases; 2 globes.
Area specialization: United States.
Special cartographic collection: gazetteers printed in U.S. prior to 1876.
Serves: Society; students.
Interlibrary loan: not available.
Reproduction facilities: photocopy; Xerox; microfilm.

261 CLARK UNIVERSITY, SCHOOL OF GEOGRAPHY. (01610) Tel. 617/793-7321. George F. McCleary, Jr., Assistant Professor.
Staff: 4 part time.
Size: 50,000 maps; 100 relief models; 200 aerial photographs; 50 gazetteers.
Annual accessions: 1,000 maps; 5 relief models; 50 aerial photographs.
Area specialization: Caribbean America.
Subject specialization: economic geography.
Depository for: TOPOCOM; USGS (topo, geol).
Serves: University; public.

MICHIGAN

Ann Arbor

262 INSTITUTE FOR FISHERIES RESEARCH, LIBRARY, Museums Annex. (48104) Tel. 313/663-3554. Margaret McClure, Libn.
Staff: 1 part time.
Size: 2,600 maps.
Area specialization: Michigan.
Subject specialization: inland lake maps.
Serves: Institute; public.
Interlibrary loan: not available.

263 UNIVERSITY OF MICHIGAN, GENERAL LIBRARY, MAP COLLECTION. (48104) Tel. 313/764-0407. Mrs. Mary K. De Vries, Map Libn.

Staff: 3 part time.
Size: 122,000 maps; 754 atlases; 10 relief models; 660 aerial photographs; 247 gazetteers.
Annual accessions: 4,500 maps; 35 atlases; 20 gazetteers.
Area specializations: Michigan; Japan.
Subject specializations: historical geography; soil surveys.
Depository for: TOPOCOM; USGS (topo, geol); USC&GS (nautical charts).
Serves: University; public.
Interlibrary loan: not available.
Reproduction facilities: photocopy; Xerox; microfilm.

264 UNIVERSITY OF MICHIGAN, MICHIGAN HISTORICAL COLLECTIONS, 160 Rackham Building. (48104) Ida C. Brown, Libn.
Size: 1,562 maps; 150 atlases.
Area specialization: Michigan.
Subject specializations: geology; mining; railroads.
Interlibrary loan: not available.
Reproduction facilities: photocopy; Xerox.

265 UNIVERSITY OF MICHIGAN, WILLIAM L. CLEMENTS LIBRARY, MAP DIVISION. (48104) Tel. 313/764-2347. Nathaniel N. Shipton, Map and Print Libn.
Staff: 1 full time.
Size: 40,000 maps; 328 atlases; 4 globes; 27 gazetteers.
Annual accessions: 20 maps.
Area specialization: United States.
Subject specializations: exploration; travel; colonial wars, and American Revolution.
Special cartographic collections: Thomas Gage Maps—Colonial Period; Henry Clinton Maps—American Revolution; Henry Vignaud Maps—17th to 19th century maps relating to America; Baldwin Maps—town surveys, canals, etc.
Serves: graduate students; public.
Interlibrary loan: not available.
Reproduction facilities: photocopy; Xerox; microfilm.
Publications: Guide to the Manuscript Maps in the William L. Clements Library by Christian Brun, Ann Arbor, 1959; *Clinton Collection: British Headquarters Maps* by R. G. Adams, Ann Arbor, 1928.

Detroit

266 DETROIT PUBLIC LIBRARY, BURTON HISTORICAL COLLECTION, 5201 Woodward Avenue. (48202) Tel. 313/321-1000, ext. 340. Mrs. Bernice C. Sprenger, Chief.
Size: 5,500 maps; 250 atlases.
Area specializations: Michigan; Great Lakes.
Serves: public.
Interlibrary loan: not available.
Reproduction facility: Xerox.

267 DETROIT PUBLIC LIBRARY, HISTORY AND TRAVEL DEPARTMENT, 5201 Woodward Avenue. (48202) Tel. 313/321-1000, ext. 263. Dorothy Starr, Map Specialist.
Staff: 1 full time; 5 part time.
Size: 119,000 maps; 2,000 atlases; 8 globes; 20 relief models; 600 gazetteers.
Annual accessions: 5,000 maps; 100 atlases; 10 gazetteers.

Area specializations: Detroit; Michigan; Canada.
Subject specializations: topography; roads; cities.
Depository for: TOPOCOM; USGS (topo, geol).
Serves: public.
Interlibrary loan: not available.
Reproduction facility: Xerox.

268 DETROIT REGIONAL TRANSPORTATION AND LAND USE STUDY, 1248 Washington Boulevard. (48226) Tel. 313/965-7480, ext. 51. Carol P. Kennedy, Regional Planner.
Staff: 2 part time.
Size: 3,000 maps; 1,500 aerial photographs.
Annual accessions: 100 maps.
Area specialization: southeastern Michigan.
Subject specializations: land use; traffic surveys.
Serves: public.
Interlibrary loan: not available.
Reproduction facility: Xerox.

269 WAYNE STATE UNIVERSITY, UNIVERSITY LIBRARIES, MAP COLLECTION. (48202) Tel. 313/833-1400, ext 510. Margaret U. Ross, Assistant Libn.
Staff: 1 part time.
Size: 34,000 maps; 575 atlases; 7 globes; 20 relief models; 200 gazetteers.
Annual accessions: 1,400 maps; 25 atlases.
Area specialization: United States.
Subject specialization: topography.
Depository for: USGS (topo).
Serves: University; public.
Interlibrary loan: available.
Reproduction facility: Xerox.

East Lansing

270 MICHIGAN STATE UNIVERSITY, LIBRARY. (48823) Tel. 517/353-4593. Mrs. Hickok, Reference Department.
Staff: 1 full time; 5 part time.
Size: 33,400 maps; 900 atlases; 2 globes; 106 gazetteers.
Annual accessions: 3,300 maps; 90 atlases.
Area specializations: United States; Latin America; Asia; Africa.
Depository for: TOPOCOM; USGS (topo, geol); Canada.
Serves: University; public.
Interlibrary loan: available.
Reproduction facility: Xerox.

Flint

271 FLINT COMMUNITY JUNIOR COLLEGE, CHARLES STEWART MOTT LIBRARY, 1401 East Court Street. (48503) Tel. 313/CE 8-1631, ext. 435. Miss Dorothy Gae Davis, Documents Libn.
Staff: 1 full time; 1 part time.
Size: 17,809 maps; 115 atlases; 1 globe; 11 relief models; 50 aerial photographs; 95 gazetteers.
Annual accessions: 699 maps.
Subject specializations: topography; geology.

Depository for: TOPOCOM.
Serves: College; public.
Interlibrary loan: available (restricted).
Reproduction facility: photocopy.

272 THE FLINT JOURNAL, EDITORIAL LIBRARY, 200 East First Street. (48502) Tel. 313/234-7611, ext. 230. W. D. Chase, Libn.
Size: 600 maps; 25 atlases; 1 globe; 400 aerial photographs; 3 gazetteers.
Annual accessions: 50 maps; 2 atlases; 50 aerial photographs.
Area specializations: Flint; Genesee County, Michigan.
Serves: employees.
Interlibrary loan: not available.
Reproduction facility: microfilm.

Grand Rapids

273 GRAND RAPIDS PUBLIC LIBRARY, Library Plaza. (49502) Tel. 616/ GL 8-1104, ext. 35. Mrs. N. M. Bartnick, Libn.
Staff: 1 full time; 1 part time.
Size: 558 maps; 55 atlases; 10 aerial photographs; 36 gazetteers.
Area specialization: Michigan.
Subject specialization: history.
Depository for: USGS (topo—Michigan).
Serves: public.
Interlibrary loan: available.
Reproduction facilities: photocopy; Xerox.

Houghton

274 MICHIGAN TECHNOLOGICAL UNIVERSITY, LIBRARY. (49931) Tel. 906/482-1600, ext. 505. Margaret E. Carlson, Reference Libn.
Staff: 1 part time.
Size: 46,000 maps; 50 atlases; 1 globe (6 ft.); 2 gazetteers.
Annual accessions: 2,500 maps.
Area specializations: United States; Canada.
Subject specializations: geology; topography.
Depository for: TOPOCOM; USGS (topo, geol); Canada; several state geological surveys.
Serves: Universtiy; public.
Interlibrary loan: not available.
Reproduction facility: Xerox.

Kalamazoo

275 WESTERN MICHIGAN UNIVERSTIY, MAP LIBRARY. (49001) Tel. 616/383-4066. Dr. Louis Kiraldi, Map Libn.
Staff: 1 full time; 1 part time.
Size: 54,000 maps; 300 atlases; 1 globe; 10 gazetteers.
Annual accessions: 8,000 maps; 50 atlases.
Area specialization: Michigan; United States; Canada.
Subject specializations: geology; topography.
Depository for: TOPOCOM; USGS (topo, geol); USC&GS; Soil Survey; International Boundary Commission—U.S. Canada; U.S. Lake Survey.
Serves: University; public.
Interlibrary loan: available.

Lansing

276 MICHIGAN (STATE) DEPARTMENT OF EDUCATION, STATE LIBRARY DIVISION, 735 East Michigan Avenue. (48913) Tel. 517/373-0938. Raymond E. Mahoney.
Size: 1,000 Maps; 160 atlases; 70 gazetteers.
Annual accessions: 25 maps; 10 atlases; 10 gazetteers.
Area specializations: Michigan; Great Lakes.
Serves: public.
Interlibrary loan: not available.
Reproduction facilities: photocopy; microfilm.

277 MICHIGAN (STATE) DEPARTMENT OF NATURAL RESOURCES, GEOLOGICAL SURVEY DIVISION, Steven T. Mason Building. (48926) Tel. 517/373-1256. Lyle D. Taylor.
Staff: 1 part time.
Size: 1,500 maps; 25 atlases; 200 aerial photographs.
Annual accessions: 100 maps.
Area specializations: Michigan; Great Lakes.
Subject specialization: geology.
Serves: employees; public.
Reproduction facilities: photocopy; Xerox; microfilm.

278 MICHIGAN HISTORICAL COMMISSION, STATE ARCHIVES AND LIBRARY, 3405 North Logan Street. (48918) Tel. 517/373-0510 or 0512. Dennis R. Bodem, State Archivist.
Staff: 5 full time.
Size: 20,000 maps; 45 atlases; 6 gazetteers.
Area specializations: Michigan; Old Northwest Territory; Great Lakes region.
Subject specializations: history; geology; topography; transportation; conservation.
Special cartographic collections: Michigan Conservation Department, Lands and Geological Survey Division—maps relating to land survey, selection, settlement, and geology, 1800–1950; State Treasury Department, Auditor General Division—Record of County Plats, 1836–1965.
Depository for: Michigan State agencies.
Serves: public.
Interlibrary loan: not available.
Reproduction facilities: photocopy; microfilm.
Publication: Bibliography of the Printed Maps of Michigan, 1804–1880 by Louis C. Karpinski. Michigan Historical Commission, 1931.

Marquette

279 MARQUETTE COUNTY HISTORICAL SOCIETY, 213 North Front Street. (49855) Tel. 906/226-6821, Ernest H. Rankin, Executive-Secretary.
Staff: 4 part time.
Size: approx. 3,000 maps; some atlases; 9 gazetteers.
Area specializations: upper peninsula of Michigan.
Serves: qualified researchers.
Interlibrary loan: available.
Reproduction facility: Xerox.

280 NORTHERN MICHIGAN UNIVERSITY, OLSON LIBRARY, Presque Isle Avenue*. (49855) Tel. 906/255-5811, ext. 2233.
Depository for: TOPOCOM.

Mt. Pleasant

281 CENTRAL MICHIGAN UNIVERSITY, CHARLES V. PARK LIBRARY, DOCUMENTS AND MAPS DIVISION. (48858) Tel. 517/774-3414. Mrs. Caroline F. Baker, Documents Libn.
Staff: 1 part time.
Size: 500 maps; 110 atlases; 2 globes; 3 aerial photographs; 15 gazetteers.
Annual accessions: 50 maps; 10 atlases.
Area specialization: Michigan cities.
Subject specialization: geology.
Serves: University; public.
Interlibrary loan: available.
Reproduction facilities: photocopy; Xerox.

282 CENTRAL MICHIGAN UNIVERSITY, CLARKE HISTORICAL LIBRARY. (48858) Tel. 517/774-3010. John Cumming, Director.
Size: 1,000 maps; 211 atlases; 53 gazetteers.
Area specializations: Great Lakes; Michigan; Old Northwest Territory.
Subject specializations: historical cartography; local history.
Serves: University; public.
Interlibrary loan: not available.
Reproduction facilities: Xerox; microfilm.

Ypsilanti

283 EASTERN MICHIGAN UNIVERSITY, LIBRARY, MAP LIBRARY. (48197) Tel. 313/483-6100, ext. 2667. Joanne Hansen, Head, Science and Technology Division.
Staff: 2 part time.
Size: 18,540 maps; 181 atlases; 2 globes; 8 relief models; 105 gazetteers.
Annual accessions: 2,478 maps; 20 atlases; 5 gazetteers.
Depository for: TOPOCOM; USGS (topo, geol).
Serves: University; public.
Interlibrary loan: not available.
Reproduction facility: Xerox.

MINNESOTA

Collegeville

284 ST. JOHN'S UNIVERSITY, ALCUIN LIBRARY. (56321) Tel. 612/363-7761, ext. 261. Rev. Ronald Roloff, Libn.
Size: 20,000 maps; 100 atlases; 200 gazetteers.
Annual accessions: 500 maps.
Depository for: TOPOCOM.
Serves: University; public.
Interlibrary loan: available.
Reproduction facility: Xerox.

Mankato

285 MANKATO STATE COLLEGE, MEMORIAL LIBRARY, MAP ROOM. (56001) Tel. 507/389-2311. Theonilla Troumbly, Map Libn.
Staff: 1 full time; 7 part time.

Size: 10,000 maps; 25 atlases; 3 globes; 6 gazetteers.
Annual accessions: 300 maps; 15 atlases; 2 globes; 3 gazetteers.
Area specialization: Minnesota.
Depository for: TOPOCOM.
Serves: College; public.
Interlibrary loan: available.
Reproduction facilities: photocopy; Xerox; microfilm (limited use).

Minneapolis

286 MINNEAPOLIS PUBLIC LIBRARY, 300 Nicollet Mall. (55401) Tel. 612/
372-6537. Miss Martina Brown, Head, History Department.
Size: 26,000 maps; 1,000 atlases; 1 globe; 100 gazetteers.
Annual accessions: 2,000 maps; 25 atlases.
Area specializations: Minnesota; midwestern United States.
Subject specializations: local history; topography.
Depository for: USGS (topo).
Serves: public.
Interlibrary loan: not available.
Reproduction facilities: photocopy; Xerox.

287 UNIVERSITY OF MINNESOTA, GEOLOGY LIBRARY, MAP ROOM,
Room 125A Pillsbury Hall. (55455) Tel. 612/373-4052. Mary H. Taylor,
Library Assistant.
Staff: 1 part time.
Size: 60,000 maps; 1,500 aerial photographs.
Annual accessions: 3,000 maps.
Area specializations: Minnesota; midwestern United States.
Subject specializations: geology; mineral resources; topography.
Depository for: USGS (topo, geol).
Serves: University; state employees.
Interlibrary loan: not available.
Reproduction facility: Xerox.

288 UNIVERSITY OF MINNESOTA, WILSON LIBRARY, AMES LI-
BRARY OF SOUTH ASIA. (55455) Tel. 612/373-2890. Henry Scholberg,
Libn.
Staff: 2 full time.
Size: 1,400 maps; 100 atlases; 1 globe; 500 gazetteers.
Annual accessions: 50 maps; 5 atlases; 50 gazetteers.
Area specialization: South Asia.
Subject specializations: social sciences; humanities.
Serves: University; public.
Interlibrary loan: available.

289 UNIVERSITY OF MINNESOTA, WILSON LIBRARY, JAMES FORD
BELL LIBRARY. (55455) Tel. 612/373-2888. Dr. John Parker, Curator.
Staff: 3 full time; 2 part time.
Size: not reported.
Special cartographic collection: a number of maps and atlases are included in this
rare book library specializing in the history of exploration and commerce from
1400 to 1800.
Serves: University; public.
Interlibrary loan: not available.
Reproduction facilities: Xerox; microfilm.

290   UNIVERSITY OF MINNESOTA, WILSON LIBRARY, MAP DIVISION. (55455) Tel. 612/373-2825. Mrs. Mai Treude, Map Libn.
Staff: 1 full time; 1 part time.
Size: 160,000 maps; 1 globe; 100,000 aerial photographs.
Annual accessions: 5,500 maps.
Special cartographic collection: early maps of Minnesota and surrounding area.
Depository for: TOPOCOM; USGS (topo); Canada; IMW; World Aeronautical Charts; NOC; United States, Argentine, and Swedish daily weather maps.
Serves: University; public.
Interlibrary loan: not available.
Reproduction facility: Xerox.
Publication: New Acquisitions (monthly).

Northfield

291   CARLETON COLLEGE, LIBRARY. (55057) Tel. 507/645-4431, ext. 466. James H. Richards, Jr., Libn.
Staff: 1 part time.
Size: 30,000 maps; 27 atlases; 1 globe; 4 relief models; 12 gazetteers.
Depository for: TOPOCOM; USGS (topo, geol).
Serves: College; public.
Interlibrary loan: not available.
Reproduction facilities: photocopy; Xerox.

St. Paul

292   HILL REFERENCE LIBRARY, 4th Street at Market Street. (55102) Tel. 612/222-5842. Russel F. Barnes, Libn.
Size: 25,000 maps.
Subject specializations: geology; topography.
Depository for: USGS (topo, geol).
Serves: public.
Reproduction facility: photocopy.

293   ST. PAUL PUBLIC LIBRARY, REFERENCE ROOM. (55102) Tel. 612/224-3383. Mrs. Helen Fleming.
Staff: 1 full time.
Size: 2,830 maps; 1 globe.
Serves: public.
Interlibrary loan: available.
Reproduction facilities: Xerox; microfilm.

St. Peter

294   GUSTAVUS ADOLPHUS COLLEGE, DEPARTMENT OF GEOGRAPHY. (56082) Tel. 507/931-4300, ext. 236. Robert T. Moline, Assistant Professor of Geography.
Staff: 3 part time.
Size: 35,000 maps; 6 globes; 225 relief models; 1,000 aerial photographs.
Annual accessions: 700 maps; 10 relief models; 50 aerial photographs.
Area specializations: midwestern United States; Europe; East Asia.
Subject specializations: topography; climatology.
Depository for: TOPOCOM.
Serves: College; public.
Interlibrary loan: available.
Reproduction facility: Xerox.

MISSISSIPPI

Jackson

295 MISSISSIPPI (STATE) DEPARTMENT OF ARCHIVES AND HISTORY, War Memorial Building, P.O. Box 571. (39205) Tel. 601/352-5001. James F. Wooldridge, Archivist.
Size: 1,000 maps; 16 atlases; 10 gazetteers.
Area specialization: southeastern United States.
Subject specialization: history.
Serves: public.
Interlibrary loan: not available.
Reproduction facilities: photocopy; Xerox; microfilm.

296 MISSISSIPPI (STATE) GEOLOGICAL SURVEY, 2525 North West Street. Tel. 601/362-1056. Mrs. W. W. Webb.
Size: 1,000 maps.
Subject specialization: geology.
Depository for: USGS (topo).
Serves: public.
Interlibrary loan: available.
Reproduction facility: photocopy.

University

297 UNIVERSITY OF MISSISSIPPI, LIBRARY, DOCUMENTS DEPART-MENT. (38677) Tel. 601/232-6237, ext. 7. Annie E. Mills, Documents Libn.
Size: 45,000 maps; 110 gazetteers.
Annual accessions: 1,840 maps.
Area specialization: United States.
Subject specialization: topography.
Depository for: USGS (topo).
Serves: University; public.
Interlibrary loan: not available.
Reproduction facility: Xerox.

Vicksburg

298 U.S. MISSISSIPPI RIVER COMMISSION, P.O. Box 80. (39180) Tel. 601/636-1311. Mrs. Margaret Palmer.
Staff: 1 part time.
Size: 500 maps.
Area specialization: lower Mississippi River Basin.
Subject specialization: navigation and flood control.
Special cartographic collection: quadrangle maps of the area immediately bordering the Mississippi River from Cairo, Illinois to the Gulf of Mexico.
Serves: public.
Interlibrary loan: not available.
Reproduction facility: blue line prints.

MISSOURI

Columbia

299 STATE HISTORICAL SOCIETY OF MISSOURI, Corner Hitt and Lowry. (65201) Tel. 314/443-3165. Richard S. Brownlee, Director.

Size: 1,600 maps; 125 atlases; 15 gazetteers.
Annual accessions: 25 maps; 10 atlases.
Area specializations: Missouri; Louisiana Territory.
Depository for: USGS (topo, geol—Missouri).
Serves: public.
Interlibrary loan: not available.
Reproduction facility: Xerox.

300 UNIVERSITY OF MISSOURI, GEOLOGY LIBRARY, 201 Geology Building. (65201) Tel. 314/449-9241, ext. 226. Mrs. Carol Dallman, Geology Libn.
Staff: 3 part time.
Size: 50,000 maps; 21 atlases; 1 globe; 10 aerial photographs.
Annual accessions: 700 maps.
Area specializations: Missouri; United States; Canada.
Subject specializations: topography; geology.
Depository for: USGS (topo, geol); Canada.
Serves: University; public.
Interlibrary loan: not available.
Reproduction facility: Xerox.

301 UNIVERSITY OF MISSOURI, LIBRARY, SERIALS DEPARTMENT, DOCUMENTS SECTION*. (65202)
Depository for: TOPOCOM.

Kansas City

302 KANSAS CITY PUBLIC LIBRARY, DOCUMENTS DIVISION*, 311 East 12th Street. (64106) Tel. 816/BA 1-1717.
Depository for: TOPOCOM.

303 LINDA HALL LIBRARY, DOCUMENTS DIVISION*, 5109 Cherry Street. (64110) Tel. 816/EM 3-4600.
Depository for: TOPOCOM.

Rolla

304 MISSOURI (STATE) GEOLOGICAL SURVEY AND WATER RE-SOURCES, P.O. Box 250. (65401) Tel. 314/364-1752, ext. 32. Mrs. Judith A. Schiffner.
Staff: 1 full time.
Size: 11,187 maps; 30 atlases; 24,564 aerial photographs.
Annual accessions: 300 maps; 5 atlases; 200 aerial photographs.
Area specialization: Missouri.
Subject specializations: geology; mining; water resources.
Depository for: USGS (topo, geol).
Serves: public.
Interlibrary loan: available.
Reproduction facility: Xerox.

305 UNIVERSITY OF MISSOURI, DEPARTMENT OF GEOLOGY AND GEOLOGICAL ENGINEERING. (65401) Tel. 314/364-4217. Dr. A. C. Spreng, Professor of Geology.
Staff: 1 part time.
Size: 15,000 maps; 50 atlases; 3 globes; 20 relief models; 3,000 aerial photographs; 2 gazetteers.

Annual accessions: 1,000 maps; 2 atlases; 200 aerial photographs.
Subject specializations: topography; geology.
Depository for: TOPOCOM; USGS (topo, geol); Canada.
Serves: University; public.
Interlibrary loan: available.
Reproduction facilities: photocopy; Xerox.

St. Louis

306 MISSOURI HISTORICAL SOCIETY, Jefferson Memorial Building.
(63112) Tel. 314/726-2622. Mrs. Fred C. Harrington, Jr., Libn.
Size: 1,000 maps; 100 atlases; 16 gazetteers.
Area specializations: Missouri; Louisiana Territory.
Special cartographic collection: early maps of Mississippi Valley.
Depository for: USGS (geol—Missouri).
Serves: qualified researchers.
Interlibrary loan: not available.
Reproduction facilities: photocopy; Xerox.

307 ST. LOUIS MERCANTILE LIBRARY, P.O. Box 633. (63188) Tel. 314/
MA 1-0670. Mary E. Mewes, Reference Libn.
Size: 500 maps; 90 atlases; 50 gazetteers.
Area specialization: Missouri.
Depository for: USGS (topo—Missouri).
Serves: public.

308 ST. LOUIS PUBLIC LIBRARY, 1301 Olive Street. (63103) Tel. 314/CH
1-2288, ext. 222. Marie H. Roberts, Chief, Reference Department.
Staff: 2 part time.
Size: 67,640 maps; 590 atlases; 1 globe.
Annual accessions: 2,468 maps.
Subject specialization: local history.
Depository for: TOPOCOM; USGS (topo, geol); Canada.
Serves: public.
Interlibrary loan: available.
Reproduction facilities: photocopy; Xerox; microfilm.
Publication: Maps in the St. Louis Public Library by Mildred Boatman. St. Louis,
1931.

309 ST. LOUIS UNIVERSITY, THE PIUS XII MEMORIAL LIBRARY, 3655
West Pine. (63108) Tel. 314/JE 5-3300. Miss Svetlana Netchvolodoff,
Periodical and Documents Libn.
Staff: 1 part time.
Size: 69,308 maps; 30 atlases; 152 gazetteers.
Annual accessions: 2,000 maps.
Depository for: TOPOCOM; USGS (topo, geol); Canada.
Serves: University; public.
Interlibrary loan: not available.

310 U.S. AERONAUTICAL CHART AND INFORMATION CENTER, DOD
AERONAUTICAL CHART SECTION (ACDEL-3), 2nd and Arsenal.
(63118) Tel. 314/268-4559. Burnell J. Petry, Supervisory Cartographer.
Staff: 50 full time.
Size: 200,000 maps.
Annual accessions: 5,000 maps.
Area specialization: comprehensive.

Subject specialization: topography.
Special cartographic collection: ACIC (USAF) Historical Chart Collection.
Serves: Federal agencies and employees.
Interlibrary loan: available (restricted to U.S. Government agencies).

311 WASHINGTON UNIVERSITY, EARTH SCIENCE LIBRARY. (63130) Tel. 314/863-0100, ext. 4351. Mrs. Harriet K. Long, Libn.
Staff: 1 full time.
Size: 58,000 maps; 85 atlases; 1 globe; 35 gazetteers.
Annual accessions: 2,900 maps.
Area specialization: Missouri.
Depository for: TOPOCOM; USGS (topo, geol); Canada.
Serves: University; public.
Interlibrary loan: not available.

MONTANA

Billings

312 BILLINGS PUBLIC LIBRARY. (59101) Tel. 406/245-5069. Mrs. Myrtle Cooper.
Staff: 2 part time.
Size: 1,200 maps; 20 atlases; 1 globe; 1 relief model; 3 gazetteers.
Annual accessions: 50 maps; 2 atlases.
Area specializations: Montana; western United States.
Subject specializations: geology; topography.
Serves: public.
Reproduction facilities: photocopy; Xerox.

Bozeman

313 MONTANA STATE UNIVERSITY, DEPARTMENT OF EARTH SCIENCES, UNIVERSITY MAP LIBRARY. (59715) Tel. 406/587-3121, ext. 518. John K. Olson, Assistant Professor of Geography.
Staff: 1 part time.
Size: 40,000 maps; 40 atlases; 6 globes; 25,000 aerial photographs; 30 gazetteers.
Annual accessions: 1,500 maps; 5 atlases; 2,500 aerial photographs; 5 gazetteers.
Area specializations: North America; South America.
Subject specializations: topography; geology; agriculture; transportation.
Depository for: TOPOCOM; USGS (topo, geol).
Serves: University; public.
Interlibrary loan: available.

Butte

314 MONTANA COLLEGE OF MINERAL SCIENCE AND TECHNOLOGY, LIBRARY. (59701) Tel. 406/792-8321, ext. 228. Mrs. Loretta B. Peck, Libn.
Staff: 1 part time.
Size: 40,000 maps; 10 atlases; 5 relief models; 15 aerial photographs; 60 gazetteers.
Annual accessions: 500 maps; 5 gazetteers.
Area specializations: Montana; western United States.
Subject specializations: geology; topography; mining.

Depository for: TOPOCOM; USGS (topo, geol); Canada (GSC).
Serves: College.
Interlibrary loan: available.
Reproduction facilities: photocopy; Xerox; microfilm.

Great Falls

315 GREAT FALLS PUBLIC LIBRARY, 2nd Avenue North and Third Street. (59401) Tel. 406/453-0349. Mrs. Ruth Frollicher.
Staff: 1 part time.
Size: 1,500 maps; 45 atlases; 2 globes.
Area specializations: Montana; United States.
Subject specializations: history; geology; roads.
Serves: public.
Interlibrary loan: not available.
Reproduction facilities: photocopy; Xerox.

Helena

316 HELENA PUBLIC LIBRARY, 325 North Park. (59601) Tel. 406/442-2380. Mrs. S. Sermon, Loan Assistant.
Size: 500 maps; 20 atlases; 2 gazetteers.
Annual accessions: 50 maps; 3 atlases.
Area specialization: northwestern United States.
Subject specialization: geology.
Depository for: USGS (geol).
Serves: public.
Interlibrary loan: not available.
Reproduction facilities: photocopy; Xerox.

Missoula

317 UNIVERSITY OF MONTANA, LIBRARY, DOCUMENTS DEPARTMENT. (59801) Tel. 406/243-2542. Dennis L. Richards, Documents Libn.
Staff: 2 part time.
Size: 56,254 maps; 150 atlases; 2 globes; 200 gazetteers.
Annual accessions: 3,000 maps; 10 atlases; 10 gazetteers.
Area specializations: Montana; northwestern United States; Canada.
Subject specializations: history; geology; topography.
Depository for: TOPOCOM; USGS (topo, geol—Montana); Canada.
Serves: University; public.
Interlibrary loan: not available.
Reproduction facilities: Xerox; microfilm.

NEBRASKA

Lincoln

318 NEBRASKA STATE HISTORICAL SOCIETY, LIBRARY, 1500 R Street. (68506) Tel. 402/432-2793. Mrs. Louise Small, Libn.
Staff: 3 part time.
Size: 5,700 maps.
Area specialization: Great Plains.
Subject specializations: frontier history; Indians; discovery and exploration.

Serves: public (by permission).
Interlibrary loan: not available.
Reproduction facility: Xerox.

319 UNIVERSITY OF NEBRASKA, UNIVERSITY LIBRARIES. (68508) Tel. 402/472-2519. Lawrence W. Kieffer, Assistant Director of Libraries for Social Studies.
Staff: 2 part time.
Size: 30,000 maps; 224 atlases; 1 globe; 3 relief models; 13,000 aerial photographs; 23 gazetteers.
Annual accessions: 1,000 maps; 25 atlases; 100 aerial photographs; 5 gazetteers.
Area specialization: Nebraska.
Subject specialization: economic geography.
Depository for: TOPOCOM; USGS (topo, geol).
Serves: University; public.
Interlibrary loan: not available.
Reproduction facility: Xerox.
Note: A collection of approximately 10,000 flat maps and 200 wall maps is housed in the University Geography Department. The University Geological Library maintains a collection of about 125,000 maps including those deposited by the USGS.

Omaha

320 OMAHA PUBLIC LIBRARY, 1823 Harney Street. (68102) Tel. 402/342-4766. Mrs. Bernice Johns, Head, Business and Industrial Department.
Size: 23,550 maps.
Annual accessions: 930 maps.
Subject specialization: topography.
Depository for: USGS (topo).
Serves: public.
Interlibrary loan: not available.
Reproduction facility: Xerox.

NEVADA

Carson City

321 NEVADA STATE LIBRARY. (89701) Tel. 702/882-7373. Jack I. Gardner, Documents Libn.
Staff: 3 full time; 1 part time.
Size: 10,000 maps; 100 atlases; 4 globes; 10 gazetteers.
Annual accessions: 1,500 maps; 10 atlases.
Area specializations: Nevada; California; Utah.
Subject specializations: geology; history; regional planning.
Depository for: USGS (topo).
Serves: state employees; public.
Interlibrary loan: available.
Reproduction facility: Xerox.

Reno

322 NEVADA HISTORICAL SOCIETY, Box 1129. (89504) Tel. 702/784-6397. Marion Welliver, Acting Director.

Staff: 4 full time; 1 part time.
Size: 600 maps; 7 atlases; 11 aerial photographs.
Area specializations: Nevada; southwestern United States.
Subject specializations: mining; trails; history.
Serves: public.
Reproduction facility: photocopy.

323   UNIVERSITY OF NEVADA, LIBRARY. (89507) Tel. 702/784-6508. Miss Helen Poulton, Reference Libn.; Mrs. Joyce Ball, Government Publications Libn.; Mrs. Constance Clark, Mines Libn.

Size: 75,300 maps.
Annual accessions: 2,600 maps.
Subject specializations: geology; geography; topography.
Special cartographic collection: Comstock Mining Maps.
Depository for: TOPOCOM; USGS (topo, geol); Canada (GSC).
Serves: University; public.
Interlibrary loan: available.
Reproduction facilities: Xerox; microfilm.
Note: The Mines Library has the USGS topographic and geologic map depository collection, state and Canadian geological surveys, and other geologic and general maps. The Government Publications Department has the TOPOCOM depository collection. The Reference Department has the major collection of atlases and gazetteers.

NEW HAMPSHIRE

Concord

324   NEW HAMPSHIRE HISTORICAL SOCIETY, 30 Park Street. (03301) Tel. 603/225-3381. Mrs. Russel B. Tobey, Libn.

Size: 350 maps; 50 atlases; 35 gazetteers.
Area specialization: New England.
Subject specialization: history.
Special cartographic collection: manuscript and printed maps of New Hampshire towns and cities.
Serves: public.
Interlibrary loan: not available.
Reproduction facilities: photocopy; Xerox.
Publication: The New Hampshire Historical Society (brochure).

325   NEW HAMPSHIRE STATE LIBRARY, 20 Park Street. (03301) Tel. 603/225-6611, ext. 425.

Size: limited.
Area specialization: New Hampshire.
Depository for: USGS (geol—selective).
Serves: public.
Interlibrary loan: available.
Reproduction facility: Xerox.

Hanover

326   DARTMOUTH COLLEGE, BAKER MEMORIAL LIBRARY, MAP ROOM. (03755) Tel. 603/646-2579. Mrs. Genevieve Lind, Reference Assistant.

Staff: 2 full time; 1 part time.
Size: 79,000 maps; 1,600 atlases; 20 globes; 335 relief models.
Annual accessions: 3,164 maps; 200 atlases.
Area specializations: New England; United States; USSR.
Subject specialization: historical cartography.
Depository for: TOPOCOM; USGS (topo, geol); Canada.
Serves: College; public.
Interlibrary loan: available (restricted).
Reproduction facilities: photocopy; Xerox.
Publication: A Brief Summary of the Resources in the Map Room in Baker Library.

Manchester

327 MANCHESTER CITY LIBRARY, 405 Pine Street. (03104) Tel. 603/625-6485. Mrs. Emily Gile, Reference Libn.
Staff: 3 part time.
Size: 1,000 maps; 50 atlases; 6 globes; 12 gazetteers.
Annual accessions: 50 maps; 5 atlases.
Area specializations: New Hampshire; New England.
Subject specialization: local history.
Depository for: USGS (topo, geol).
Serves: public.
Interlibrary loan: not available.
Reproduction facilities: photocopy; microfilm.

328 MANCHESTER HISTORIC ASSOCIATION, 129 Amherst Street. (03102) Tel. 603/662-7531. Mrs. Elizabeth Lessard, Libn.
Staff: 1 full time.
Size: 2,488 maps; 2 globes; 2 aerial photographs; 2 gazetteers.
Area specializations: Manchester; New Hampshire.
Subject specializations: history; canals.
Serves: members; public (by permission).
Interlibrary loan: not available.
Reproduction facility: photocopy.

NEW JERSEY

Bloomfield

329 BLOOMFIELD PUBLIC LIBRARY, 90 Broad Street. (07003) Tel. 201/743-7875, ext. 31. Mrs. Dorothy E. Johnson, Reference Libn.
Size: 800 maps; 56 atlases; 1 globe; 1 aerial photograph; 3 gazetteers.
Area specialization: New Jersey.
Subject specialization: local history.
Special cartographic collection: small collection of early Bloomfield, N.J., maps on microfilm.
Serves: public.
Interlibrary loan: available (restricted).
Reproduction facilities: Xerox; microfilm.

Convent Station

330 GENERAL DRAFTING COMPANY, INC., Canfield Road. (07961) Tel. 201/538-7600, ext. 56. Frederic R. Parker, Libn.

Staff: 1 full time; 1 part time.
Size: 75,000 maps; 50 atlases; 25 globes; 100 relief models; 10 aerial photographs; 500 gazetteers.
Area specializations: United States; Canada; Latin America.
Subject specializations: highways; educational materials; geography.
Serves: employees.
Interlibrary loan: available (restricted).

East Orange

331 EAST ORANGE PUBLIC LIBRARY, 221 Freeway Drive East. (07018) Tel. 201/677-3700, ext. 15. Marc M. Eisen, Reference Libn.
Staff: 1 part time.
Size: 3,000 maps; 85 atlases; 1 globe; 3 gazetteers.
Area specializations: East Orange; New Jersey.
Subject specializations: local history; geology.
Serves: public.
Interlibrary loan: not available.
Reproduction facility: photocopy.

Glassboro

332 GLASSBORO STATE COLLEGE, SAVITZ LIBRARY. STEWART COLLECTION. (08208) Tel. 609/881-8400, ext. 341. Professor Magdalena Houlroyd, Curator.
Staff: 1 part time.
Size: 243 maps; 16 atlases.
Area specialization: New Jersey.
Subject specialization: local history.
Special cartographic collection: maps and atlases listed here are part of the Stewart Collection of Jerseyana which also includes early deeds and land surveys.
Serves: College; public.
Interlibrary loan: not available.
Reproduction facility: Xerox.

Jersey City

333 JERSEY CITY PUBLIC LIBRARY, GENERAL REFERENCE DEPARTMENT, SPECIAL COLLECTIONS DIVISION, 472 Jersey Avenue. Tel. 201/435-6262, ext. 11A. Robert Lagerstrom, Principal Reference Libn.
Staff: 1 part time.
Size: approximately 400 maps; 50 atlases; 12 gazetteers.
Annual accessions: 200 maps; 12 atlases.
Area specialization: New Jersey.
Subject specialization: local history.
Serves: public.
Interlibrary loan: not available.
Reproduction facilities: photocopy; Xerox.

Maplewood

334 HAMMOND INC., EDITORIAL DIVISION LIBRARY, 515 Valley Street. (07040) Tel. 201/763-3000. Martin A. Bacheller, Vice President and Editor-in-Chief.
Staff: 1 full time; 1 part time.

Size: 12,000 maps; 400 atlases; 5 globes; 5 relief models; 250 gazetteers.
Annual accessions: 500 maps; 50 atlases; 25 gazetteers.
Subject specializations: geography; demography.
Serves: employees.
Interlibrary loan: not available.
Reproduction facilities: photocopy; Xerox.

Newark

335   NEW JERSEY HISTORICAL SOCIETY, LIBRARY, 230 Broadway.
(07104) Tel. 201/483-3939. Mrs. Edith O. May, Libn.
Staff: 2 full time; 1 part time.
Size: 1,000 maps; 50 atlases.
Area specialization: New Jersey.
Serves: public.
Interlibrary loan: not available.
Reproduction facilities: photocopy; Xerox; microfilm.

336   NEWARK PUBLIC LIBRARY, 5 Washington Street. (07101) Tel. 201/
624-7100, ext. 255. Mrs. Ruth Challender, Senior Libn.
Staff: 5 part time.
Size: 16,000 maps; 600 atlases; 150 gazetteers.
Annual accessions: 800 maps.
Depository for: USGS (topo).
Serves: public.
Interlibrary loan: not available.
Reproduction facilities: photocopy; Xerox.

New Brunswick

337   RUTGERS UNIVERSITY, LIBRARY, GOVERNMENT PUBLICA-
TIONS DEPARTMENT. (08901) Tel. 201/CH 7-1766, ext. 6526. Francois
X. Grondin, Chief.
Staff: 1 full time; 1 part time.
Size: 50,000 maps.
Subject specializations: geology; urban studies.
Depository for: TOPOCOM; USGS (topo, geol); Canada; USC&GS; New Jersey; United
Nations.
Serves: University; public.
Interlibrary loan: available (restricted).
Reproduction facilities: Xerox; microfilm.

Princeton

338   PRINCETON UNIVERSITY, GEOLOGY LIBRARY. (08540) Tel. 609/
452-3235. Hartley K. Phinney, Jr., Libn.
Staff: 1 full time; 3 part time.
Size: 60,000 maps; 73 atlases; 5 relief models; 5,600 aerial photographs; 17
gazetteers.
Annual accessions: 5,000 maps; 5 atlases; 600 aerial photographs.
Area specialization: United States.
Subject specializations: geology; oceanography.
Depository for: USGS (topo, geol).
Serves: University; public.
Interlibrary loan: not available.
Reproduction facilities: photocopy; microfilm.

339 PRINCETON UNIVERSITY, LIBRARY, MAP DIVISION. (08540) Tel. 609/452-3214. Lawrence E. Spellman, Curator of Maps.
Staff: 1 full time; 3 part time.
Size: 100,000 maps; 160 atlases; 8 globes; 20 relief models; 750 aerial photographs; 130 gazetteers.
Annual accessions: 7,600 maps; 20 atlases; 2 globes; 4 relief models; 15 aerial photographs; 10 gazetteers.
Area specializations: New Jersey; United States.
Subject specializations: local history; transportation.
Depository for: TOPOCOM; USGS (topo); ESSA; USAF.
Serves: University; public.
Interlibrary loan: available.
Reproduction facilities: photocopy; Xerox; microfilm.

Rutherford

340 FAIRLEIGH DICKINSON UNIVERSITY, MESSLER LIBRARY, NEW JERSEY ROOM. (07070) Tel. 201/933-5000, ext. 305. Mrs. Catharine M. Fogarty, Libn.
Staff: 1 part time.
Size: 442 maps; 33 atlases.
Area specializations: New Jersey; New York.
Serves: University; public.
Interlibrary loan: not available.
Reproduction facility: photocopy.

Trenton

341 NEW JERSEY STATE LIBRARY, BUREAU OF ARCHIVES AND HISTORY, 185 West State Street. (08625) Tel. 609/292-6209. David C. Munn, Reference Libn.
Size: 1,400 maps.
Area specialization: New Jersey.
Serves: public.
Interlibrary loan: not available.
Reproduction facility: Xerox.

342 TRENTON FREE PUBLIC LIBRARY, REFERENCE DEPARTMENT, 120 Academy Street. (08608) Tel. 609/392-7188. Mrs. J. R. Muehleck, Head.
Staff: 5 full time; 5 part time.
Size: 700 maps; 150 atlases; 25 aerial photographs; 15 gazetteers.
Area specializations: Trenton; New Jersey.
Subject specialization: local history.
Serves: public.
Interlibrary loan: not available.
Reproduction facility: photocopy.

343 TRENTON STATE COLLEGE, GEOGRAPHY DEPARTMENT, MAP LIBRARY. (08625) Tel. 609/882-1855, ext. 347. Mrs. Elizabeth Strasser, Assistant Professor.
Staff: 1 part time.
Size: 10,000 maps; 20 globes; 75 relief models; 30 aerial photographs.
Annual accessions: 150 maps; 10 relief models.
Depository for: TOPOCOM.
Serves: College.
Interlibrary loan: not available.
Reproduction facility: Xerox.

NEW MEXICO

Albuquerque

344 ALBUQUERQUE PUBLIC LIBRARY, SOUTHWEST ROOM, 423 Central Avenue, N.E. (87101) Tel. 505/243-5679. Katherine McMahon, Southwest Libn.
Staff: 3 full time; 1 part time.
Size: 2,300 maps; 50 atlases; 3 gazetteers.
Area specialization: New Mexico.
Subject specializations: geology; history; mineral resources; topography; water resources.
Serves: public.
Interlibrary loan: not available.
Reproduction facility: Xerox.

345 U.S. GEOLOGICAL SURVEY, WRD, LIBRARY, P.O. Box 4369. (87106) Tel. 505/843-2248. Mrs. Elizabeth M. Kuntz, Libn.
Staff: 1 full time.
Size: 3,000 maps; 500 atlases.
Annual accessions: 150 maps; 40 atlases.
Area specialization: southwestern United States.
Subject specializations: geology; water resources.
Depository for: USGS (topo, geol); New Mexico State Engineer and State Bureau of Mines.
Serves: public.
Interlibrary loan: available.

346 UNIVERSITY OF NEW MEXICO, ZIMMERMAN LIBRARY, SPECIAL COLLECTIONS. (87106) Tel. 505/277-4241, ext. 55. David Otis Kelly, University Libn.
Staff: 1 full time; 2 part time.
Size: 60,000 maps; 23 atlases; 22 relief models; 92 aerial photographs; 152 gazetteers.
Annual accessions: 1,500 maps; 4 atlases; 3 relief models; 10 gazetteers.
Subject specialization: topography.
Special cartographic collection: Sanborn fire insurance maps of New Mexico, 1883–1930.
Depository for: TOPOCOM; USGS (topo).
Serves: University; public.
Interlibrary loan: not available.
Reproduction facilities: photocopy; Xerox; microfilm.

Las Cruces

347 NEW MEXICO STATE UNIVERSITY, LIBRARY. (88001) Tel. 505/646-4513. Walter J. McGuire, Special Collections Libn.
Staff: 1 full time.
Size: 16,000 maps; 15 atlases; 500 aerial photographs; 5 gazetteers.
Annual accessions: 300 maps.
Area specialization: New Mexico.
Subject specializations: geology; topography.
Depository for: TOPOCOM; USGS (topo, geol).
Serves: University; public.
Interlibrary loan: not available.
Reproduction facility: Xerox.

Portales

348 EASTERN NEW MEXICO UNIVERSITY, LIBRARY. (88130) Tel. 505/ 562-2832. Mrs. Mary Anne Rangel-Guerrero, Map and Reference Libn.
Staff: 1 part time.
Size: 1,000 maps; 75 atlases; 50 relief models.
Area specialization: New Mexico.
Serves: University.
Interlibrary loan: not available.
Reproduction facility: Xerox.

Santa Fe

349 MUSEUM OF NEW MEXICO, LABORATORY OF ANTHROPOLOGY, LIBRARY, P.O. Box 2087. (87501) Tel. 505/827-2732. Mary M. Bryan, Libn.
Staff: 1 part time.
Size: 2,500 maps.
Area specialization: New Mexico.
Subject specialization: topography.
Depository for: USGS (topo).
Serves: students.
Interlibrary loan: not available.

350 NEW MEXICO STATE LIBRARY, P.O. Box 1629. (87501) Tel. 505/827-2103. Virginia Jennings, Libn.
Size: 700 maps; 2 atlases.
Annual accessions: 25 maps.
Area specialization: southwestern United States.
Subject specialization: local history.
Serves: public.
Interlibrary loan: not available.
Reproduction facility: Xerox.

Taos

351 KIT CARSON MEMORIAL FOUNDATION, HISTORICAL RE-SEARCH LIBRARY, P.O. Box 398. (87571) Jack K. Boyer, Director.
Staff: 1 part time.
Size: 289 maps; 5 atlases; 2 relief models; 5 aerial photographs.
Annual accessions: 20 maps.
Area specializations: New Mexico; trans-Mississippi West.
Subject specializations: early fur trade; Kit Carson; local history.
Serves: public.
Interlibrary loan: not available.

NEW YORK

Albany

352 NEW YORK STATE DEPARTMENT OF TRANSPORTATION, MAP INFORMATION UNIT, State Campus. (12226) Tel. 518/457-4755. Paul McElligott, Senior Cartographer.
Staff: 5 part time.
Size: 4,000 maps; 60 atlases; 10 relief models; 20,000 aerial photographs; 5 gazetteers.

Area specialization: New York State.
Special cartographic collections: 600 patent boundary maps of New York State, 1780-1850; 60 New York State county atlases, 1859-1900.
Depository for: New York State Department of Transportation.
Serves: employees; other State agencies.
Interlibrary loan: available.
Reproduction facilities: photocopy; Xerox; microfilm; Diazo.

353 NEW YORK STATE LIBRARY, MANUSCRIPTS AND HISTORY LIBRARY. (12224) Tel. 518/474-5963. Juliet F. Wolohan, Associate Libn.
Staff: 4 part time.
Size: 60,000 maps; 830 atlases; 45 gazetteers.
Area specializations: New York State; United States.
Subject specializations: history; topography; geology; transportation.
Depository for: TOPOCOM; USGS (topo, geol); other State agencies.
Serves: public.
Interlibrary loan: available (restricted).
Reproduction facilities: photocopy; Xerox; microfilm.

Binghamton

354 STATE UNIVERSITY OF NEW YORK AT BINGHAMTON, DEPARTMENT OF GEOLOGY. (13901) Tel. 607/798-2265. Dr. Donald R. Coates, Professor of Geology.
Staff: 2 part time.
Size: 50,000 maps; 1,500 atlases; 2 globes; 200 relief models; 750 aerial photographs.
Annual accessions: 2,600 maps; 100 atlases; 50 aerial photographs.
Subject specialization: geology.
Depository for: USGS (topo, geol).
Serves: University; public.
Interlibrary loan: available.
Reproduction facility: Xerox.

Blue Mountain Lake

355 ADIRONDACK MUSEUM. (12812) Tel. 518/352-7311. Marcia Smith, Libn.
Size: 500 maps.
Area specialization: Adirondack region.

Brooklyn

356 BROOKLYN PUBLIC LIBRARY, HISTORY DIVISION, MAP COLLECTION, Grand Army Plaza. (11238) Tel. 212/ST 9-1212, ext. 732. Mr. Tsugio Yoshinaga, Libn.
Staff: 2 part time.
Size: 65,000 maps; 750 atlases; 2 globes; 5 relief models; 30 aerial photographs; 200 gazetteers.
Annual accessions: 4,000 maps; 25 atlases; 15 gazetteers.
Area specializations: Brooklyn; New York State.
Subject specializations: local history; topography; U.S. city street guides.
Depository for: TOPOCOM; USGS (topo).
Serves: public.

Interlibrary loan: not available.
Reproduction facilities: photocopy; Xerox; microfilm.

357　LONG ISLAND HISTORICAL SOCIETY, 128 Pierrepont Street. (11201) Tel. 212/MA 4-0890. John H. Lindenbusch, Executive Director.
Staff: 2 part time.
Size: 1,600 maps; 300 atlases; 100 aerial photographs; 100 gazetteers.
Area specialization: Long Island.
Serves: public.
Interlibrary loan: not available.
Reproduction facility: photocopy.

Buffalo

358　BUFFALO AND ERIE COUNTY HISTORICAL SOCIETY, 25 Nottingham Court. (14225) Tel. 716/873-9644. Paul F. Redding, Curator of Iconography.
Staff: 1 full time; 1 part time.
Size: 3,000 maps; 75 atlases; 4,500 aerial photographs; 12 gazetteers.
Annual accessions: 25 maps; 50 aerial photographs.
Area specializations: Buffalo; Erie County; New York State.
Subject specialization: local history.
Serves: public.
Interlibrary loan: available.
Reproduction facilities: photocopy; Xerox; microfilm.

359　BUFFALO AND ERIE COUNTY PUBLIC LIBRARY, HISTORY, TRAVEL AND GOVERNMENT DEPARTMENT, Lafayette Square. (14203) Tel. 716/856-7525. Miss Evelyn L. Hess, Libn.
Staff: 1 part time.
Size: 45,000 maps; 300 atlases; 1 globe; 1 aerial photograph; 100 gazetteers.
Annual accessions: 1,600 maps; 10 atlases; 4 gazetteers.
Area specialization: Buffalo.
Subject specializations: local history; topography; transportation; political geography.
Special cartographic collection: portolan charts (in Rare Book Room).
Depository for: TOPOCOM; USGS (topo, geol).
Serves: public.
Interlibrary loan: not available.
Reproduction facility: Xerox.

Clinton

360　HAMILTON COLLEGE, DEPARTMENT OF GEOLOGY, MAP LIBRARY. (13323) Tel. 315/853-5511, ext. 226. David Hawley, Professor of Geology.
Staff: 1 part time.
Size: 30,000 maps; 70 atlases; 20 relief models; 200 aerial photographs.
Annual accessions: 1,000 maps.
Area specializations: North America; Africa; Europe; Asia.
Subject specializations: topography; geology.
Depository for: USGS (topo, geol).
Serves: College; public (by permission).
Interlibrary loan: not available.

Hamilton

361   COLGATE UNIVERSITY, GEOGRAPHY DEPARTMENT*. (13346) Tel. 315/824-1000, ext. 218.

Depository for: TOPOCOM.

Ithaca

362   CORNELL UNIVERSITY, CENTER FOR AERIAL PHOTOGRAPHIC STUDIES, INTERNATIONAL AERIAL PHOTOGRAPHIC LIBRARY. (14850) Tel. 607/275-3684. Donald J. Belcher, Director.

Staff: 2 part time.
Size: 700,000 aerial photographs.
Annual accessions: 20,000 aerial photographs.
Area specialization: worldwide.
Subject specializations: agriculture; engineering; regional and urban planning; geology.
Serves: University; public.
Interlibrary loan: available.

363   CORNELL UNIVERSITY, JOHN M. OLIN LIBRARY, DEPARTMENT OF MAPS, MICROTEXTS AND NEWSPAPERS. (14850) Tel. 607/275-5258. Barbara Berthelsen, Map Libn.

Staff: 1 full time; 8 part time.
Size: 81,000 maps; 1,000 atlases; 7 globes; 28 relief models; 110 gazetteers.
Annual accessions: 5,500 maps.
Area specializations: New York State; Latin America; Indonesia; China; Far East.
Subject specializations: local history; geology; transportation; urban geography.
Special cartographic collection: Wason Far East Collection.
Depository for: TOPOCOM; USGS (topo, geol).
Serves: University; public.
Interlibrary loan: not available.
Reproduction facilities: photocopy; Xerox.

Jamaica

364   QUEENS BOROUGH PUBLIC LIBRARY, HISTORY, TRAVEL AND BIOGRAPHY DIVISION, 89-11 Merrick Boulevard. (11432) Tel. 212/739-1900, ext. 256. Mrs. Margaret F. Clark, Division Head.

Size: 2,150 maps; 178 atlases; 17 gazetteers.
Area specializations: New York State; United States.
Subject specialization: transportation.
Serves: public.
Interlibrary loan: available.
Reproduction facility: photocopy.

365   QUEENS BOROUGH PUBLIC LIBRARY, LONG ISLAND DIVISION, 89-11 Merrick Boulevard. (11432) Tel. 212/739-1900, ext. 215. Davis Erhardt, Division Head.

Size: 5,000 maps; 125 atlases; 150 aerial photographs; 25 gazetteers.
Area specializations: New York State; Long Island.
Subject specialization: local history.
Serves: public.
Interlibrary loan: not available.
Reproduction facility: photocopy.

366   AMERICAN ALPINE CLUB, 113 E. 90th Street. (10028) Tel. 212/722-1628. Margot McKee, Libn.
Staff: 1 part time.
Size: 1,000 maps; 25 atlases; 10 relief models; 5 gazetteers.
Annual accessions: 150 maps.
Subject specialization: mountains; mountaineering.
Serves: public.
Interlibrary loan: not available.

367   AMERICAN GEOGRAPHICAL SOCIETY, MAP DEPARTMENT, Broadway at 156th Street. (10032) Tel. 212/AD 4-8100, ext. 6 and 15. Dr. Roman Drazniowsky, Map Curator.
Staff: 4 full time; 2 part time.
Size: 310,000 maps; 4,700 atlases; 50 globes; 600 gazetteers.
Annual accessions: 9,000 maps; 150 atlases; 3 globes; 10 gazetteers.
Area specializations: comprehensive; North America; South America.
Subject specialization: comprehensive.
Depository for: TOPOCOM; USGS (topo, geol); Canada; Great Britain; Australia.
Serves: public.
Interlibrary loan: available
Reproduction facility: Xerox.
Publications: Current Geographical Publications, Section Three (selected maps and atlases); *Cataloging and Filing Rules for Maps and Atlases in the Society's Collection.* Mimeographed and offset Publications No. 4, 1964. Revised.

368   COLUMBIA UNIVERSITY, UNIVERSITY MAP ROOM, 601 Schermerhorn Building. (10027) Tel. 212/280-4520. Albert J. Takazauckas, Map Room Attendant.
Staff: 1 full time; 2 part time.
Size: 150,000 maps; 50 atlases; 9 globes; 14 relief models.
Annual accessions: 4,000 maps; 5 relief models.
Area specialization: North America.
Subject specialization: earth sciences.
Depository for: TOPOCOM; USGS (topo, geol); Canada.
Serves: University; public (by permission).
Interlibrary loan: available (very restricted).
Reproduction facility: Xerox.

369   ENGINEERING SOCIETIES LIBRARY, 345 East 47th Street. (10017) Tel. 212/752-6800.
Size: 10,000 maps; 20 atlases; 60 gazetteers.
Annual accessions: 275 maps.
Area specialization: United States.
Subject specializations: geology; terrestrial and aeromagnetism.
Depository for: USGS (geol).
Serves: public.
Interlibrary loan: not available.
Reproduction facilities: Xerox; microfilm.

370   EXPLORERS CLUB, 46 East 70th Street. (10021) Tel. 212/628-8385, ext. 5. Roy Fentress, Libn.
Staff: 1 full time; 2 part time.
Size: 5,000 maps; 150 atlases; 3 globes.

Annual accessions: 200 maps.
Subject specializations: discovery and exploration; expedition routes.
Serves: public.
Interlibrary loan: available.
Reproduction facility: photocopy.

371   HISPANIC SOCIETY OF AMERICA, 613 West 155th Street. (10032)
Size: approximately 50 maps; 27 globes. (Data from *Directory of Map Collections
   . . .,* 1954)
Area specializations: Spain; Portugal; South and Central America.
Special cartographic collection: 42 manuscript maps including 32 portolan charts.
Serves: public.

372   MISSIONARY RESEARCH LIBRARY, 3041 Broadway. (10027) Tel. 212/
662-7100, ext. 415. Anson Huang, Assistant Director.
Size: 596 maps; 136 atlases.
Subject specialization: Christian missions.
Serves: public.
Interlibrary loan: available.

373   NEW YORK HISTORICAL SOCIETY, MAP AND PRINT ROOM, 170
Central Park West. (10024) Tel. 212/873-3400. Wilson G. Duprey, Curator.
Staff: 2 full time.
Size: not reported.
Area specializations: New York City and State.
Subject specialization: history.
Serves: public.
Interlibrary loan: not available.
Reproduction facility: photocopy.

374   NEW YORK PUBLIC LIBRARY, MAP DIVISION, Fifth Avenue and
42nd Street. (10018) Tel. 212/790-6286. Gerard L. Alexander, Chief, Map
Division.
Staff: 5 full time; 2 part time.
Size: 287,202 maps; 5,941 atlases; 5 globes; 600 gazetteers.
Annual accessions: 4,000 maps; 200 atlases; 10 gazetteers.
Area specialization: comprehensive.
Subject specialization: history of cartography.
Special cartographic collections: rare 17th and 18th century atlases and maps;
   United States county and real estate atlases; map collections of James Lenox,
   I.N. Phelps Stokes, and others.
Depository for: TOPOCOM; USGS (topo, geol); Canada.
Serves: public.
Interlibrary loan: not available.
Reproduction facilities: photocopy; Xerox; microfilm.
Publications: occasional lists, articles and bibliographical studies in the New York
   Public Library *Bulletin.*
Note: The Rare Book Division (Mr. Lewis M. Stark, Chief) has custody of many
   rare cartographic works including maps, atlases, globes, and globe gores.

**375   UNITED NATIONS, DAG HAMMARSKJOLD LIBRARY, MAP COL-
LECTION.** (10017) Tel. 212/PL 4-1234, ext. 834. Nathaniel O. Abelson,
Map Libn.
Staff: 2 full time.
Size: 75,000 maps; 800 atlases; 3 globes; 25 relief models; 1,075 gazetteers.
Annual accessions: 3,000 maps.

Subject specializations: topography; geology; transportation; toponymy; political geography.
Special cartographic collection: maps of armistice and cease-fire lines.
Serves: United Nations; qualified researchers.
Interlibrary loan: not available.
Reproduction facilities: photocopy; Xerox; microfilm; Ozalid.

Ossining

376 OSSINING HISTORICAL SOCIETY MUSEUM, 83 Croton Avenue. (10562) Miss Greta Cornell, Director.
Staff: 1 full time; 5 part time.
Size: 330 maps; 21 atlases; 1 globe; 4 aerial photographs; 1 gazetteer.
Area specializations: Ossining; Westchester County.
Subject specialization: local history.
Serves: public.
Interlibrary loan: not available.

Potsdam

377 STATE UNIVERSITY COLLEGE, FREDERICK W. CRUMB MEMORIAL LIBRARY. (13676) Tel. 315/268-4955. Mrs. Alice F. Kauffman, Documents Libn.
Staff: 2 part time.
Size: 1,803 maps; 149 atlases; 3 globes.
Area specialization: New York State.
Subject specializations: geology; topography.
Serves: College; public.
Interlibrary loan: available.
Reproduction facility: Xerox.

Poughkeepsie

378 VASSAR COLLEGE, DEPARTMENT OF GEOLOGY AND GEOGRAPHY*. (12601).
Depository for: TOPOCOM.

Rochester

379 UNIVERSITY OF ROCHESTER, GEOLOGICAL SCIENCES LIBRARY AND MAP CENTER, Dewey Building, River Campus. (14627) Tel. 716/275-4487. Mrs. Suzette Giles, Library Assistant.
Staff: 1 full time; 1 part time.
Size: 45,300 maps; 42 atlases; 6 relief models.
Annual accessions: 3,900 maps.
Area specializations: New York State; Pennsylvania.
Subject specialization: geology.
Depository for: USGS (topo, geol); Canada; USC&GS (coast and harbor charts, aeronautical charts).
Serves: University; public.
Interlibrary loan: not available.
Reproduction facilities: photocopy; Xerox.

Staten Island

380 STATEN ISLAND INSTITUTE OF ARTS AND SCIENCES, LIBRARY, MAP COLLECTION, 75 Stuyvesant Place, St. George. (10301) Tel. 212/727-1135. Mrs. G. K. Schneider, Editor/Librarian.

Staff: 1 full time.

Size: approximately 1,300 maps; 40 atlases; 5 aerial photographs; 11 gazetteers.

Area specializations: New York State; Europe.

Subject specializations: European history 1600–1800; city maps.

Special cartographic collection: Sanderson Smith Collection of historical maps of Europe and Asia.

Depository for: USGS (topo, geol).

Interlibrary loan: not available.

Publication: The Collection of Prints, Drawings, Maps, and Photographs in the Library of the Staten Island Institute of Arts and Sciences (in preparation). *Map of Staten Island . . . Ye Olde Names and Nicknames* (22½" × 31").

Syracuse

381 SYRACUSE UNIVERSITY, NATURAL SCIENCES LIBRARY, 407 Lyman Hall. (13210). Tel. 315/476-5541, ext. 2160. Mrs. Jessie Watkins, Branch Libn.

Staff: 1 full time.

Size: 75,000 maps; 475 atlases; 1 globe; 110 gazetteers.

Area specialization: United States.

Subject specialization: topography.

Depository for: TOPOCOM; USGS (topo, geol).

Serves: University.

Interlibrary loan: not available.

Reproduction facility: Xerox.

Utica

382 UTICA PUBLIC LIBRARY, 303 Genesee Street. (13501). Tel. 315/735-2279.

Size: 2,155 maps; 59 atlases; 2 globes.

Area specializations: Utica; Oneida County; New York State; United States.

Subject specialization: local history.

Serves: public.

Interlibrary loan: available (restricted).

Reproduction facilities: photocopy; Xerox; microfilm.

West Point

383 U.S. MILITARY ACADEMY, DEPARTMENT OF EARTH, SPACE AND GRAPHIC SCIENCES, MAP LIBRARY. (10996) Tel. 914/938-2302. Charles E. Nikola, Map Libn.

Staff: 1 full time.

Size: 60,000 maps; 50 atlases; 2,000 relief models; 20 gazetteers.

Annual accessions: 5,000 maps.

Area specializations: United States; USSR; Latin America.

Subject specialization: topography.

Special cartographic collection: historical maps of West Point and vicinity from the Revolution to the present.

Depository for: TOPOCOM.

Serves: Academy; qualified researchers.
Interlibrary loan: not available.
Reproduction facility: photocopy.

384   U.S. MILITARY ACADEMY, LIBRARY. (10996) Tel. 914/938-2954.
Staff: 1 full time.
Size: 500 maps; 50 atlases; 2 globes; 1 relief model; 50 aerial photographs.
Area specialization: New York.
Subject specialization: military history.
Special cartographic collection: Civil War Confederate—Izard Collection.
Serves: Academy; qualified researchers.
Interlibrary loan: not available.

385   U.S. MILITARY ACADEMY, LIBRARY, SPECIAL COLLECTIONS
DIVISION. (10996) Tel. 914/938-2954. Dr. Edward P. Rich, Special
Collections Libn.
Staff: 1 full time.
Size: 2,000 maps; 500 atlases; 3 globes.
Area specializations: United States; Europe.
Subject specialization: military history.
Special cartographic collection: Gilmer Collection (Civil War—Confederate States
of America).
Serves: Academy; qualified researchers.
Interlibrary loan: not available.
Reproduction facility: Xerox.

NORTH CAROLINA

Buie's Creek

386   CAMPBELL COLLEGE, CARRIE RICH MEMORIAL LIBRARY, MAP
DIVISION. (27506) Tel. 919/893-4111. Rick Jones, Map Curator.
Staff: 1 part time.
Size: 3,000 maps; 25 atlases; 2 globes; 5 relief models; 1 aerial photograph.
Area specialization: eastern United States.
Subject specializations: topography; geology.
Depository for: USGS (topo, geol).
Serves: College; public.
Interlibrary loan: not available.
Reproduction facilities: photocopy; Xerox; microfilm.

Chapel Hill

387   UNIVERSITY OF NORTH CAROLINA, DEPARTMENT OF GEOL-
OGY, LIBRARY. (27514) Tel. 919/933-2386. Mrs. Dolores H. Swindell,
Libn.
Staff: 1 full time; 2 part time.
Size: 41,000 maps; 200 atlases; 1 globe.
Area specialization: southeastern United States.
Subject specializations: geology; topography.
Depository for: USGS (topo,geol); Canada.
Serves: University; public.
Interlibrary loan: available.
Reproduction facilities: photocopy; Xerox; microfilm.

388 UNIVERSITY OF NORTH CAROLINA, LIBRARY, MAP ROOM. (27514) Louise McG. Hall, Head, Humanities Division.
Staff: 1 full time; 2 part time.
Size: 64,000 maps; 750 atlases; 110 relief models.
Area specializations: North Carolina; southeastern United States.
Subject specializations: local history.
Depository for: TOPOCOM.
Serves: University; public.
Reproduction facilities: photocopy; Xerox; microfilm.
Note: North Carolina Collection included in map statistics.

Durham

389 DUKE UNIVERSITY, LIBRARY, PUBLIC DOCUMENTS DEPARTMENT. (27706) Tel. 919/684-2380. Wilhelmina Lemen, Documents Libn.
Staff: 1 part time.
Size: 46,650 maps; 105 gazetteers.
Annual accessions: 2,400 maps.
Depository for: TOPOCOM; USGS (topo, geol).
Serves: University; public.
Interlibrary loan: available (restricted).
Reproduction facility: Xerox.

Greenville

390 EAST CAROLINA UNIVERSITY, DEPARTMENT OF GEOGRAPHY, MAP LIBRARY, Box 2723. (27834) Tel. 919/758-3426, ext. 256. Dr. Robert E. Cramer, Department Chairman.
Size: 12,776 maps; 5 atlases; 6 globes; 40 relief models; 10,000 aerial photographs; 10 gazetteers.
Annual accessions: 1,000 maps; 2 atlases; 5 relief models; 3,000 aerial photographs.
Area specialization: United States.
Subject specialization: topography.
Depository for: TOPOCOM; USGS (topo).
Serves: University; public.
Interlibrary loan: not available.

Raleigh

391 NORTH CAROLINA (STATE) DEPARTMENT OF ARCHIVES AND HISTORY, P.O. Box 1881. (27602) Tel. 919/829-3952. C. F. W. Coker, Assistant Archives Administrator.
Staff: 10 part time.
Size: 3,000 maps; 25 atlases; 5,000 aerial photographs; 10 gazetteers.
Annual accessions: 100 maps; 2 atlases.
Area specializations: North Carolina; southeastern United States.
Serves: public.
Interlibrary loan: not available.
Reproduction facilities: photocopy; Xerox; microfilm.
Publication: North Carolina in Maps, edited by W. P. Cumming. Division of Publications, State Department of Archives and History, Raleigh.

392 NORTH CAROLINA STATE UNIVERSITY, D. H. HILL LIBRARY.
(27607) Tel. 919/755-2844. Miss Mary Elizabeth Poole, Documents Libn.
Size: not reported.
Depository for: USGS (topo—North Carolina).
Serves: University; public.
Interlibrary loan: not available.
Reproduction facility: Xerox.

NORTH DAKOTA

Fargo

393 NORTH DAKOTA STATE UNIVERSITY, LIBRARY. (58102) Tel. 701/
237-7811.
Size: not reported.
Area specialization: North Dakota.
Subject specialization: geology.
Depository for: TOPOCOM; USGS (geol).
Serves: University; public.
Interlibrary loan: available.
Reproduction facility: Xerox.

Grand Forks

394 UNIVERSITY OF NORTH DAKOTA, GEOGRAPHY DEPARTMENT
LIBRARY. (58201) Tel. 701/777-3611. D. L. Younggren, Chairman,
Geography Department.
Size: 30,000 maps; 100 atlases; 50 globes; 150 relief models.
Annual accessions: 2,000 maps.
Depository for: TOPOCOM.
Serves: University; public.
Interlibrary loan: not available.
Reproduction facility: Xerox.

395 UNIVERSITY OF NORTH DAKOTA, GEOLOGY LIBRARY, 326
Leonard Hall. (58201) Tel. 701/777-2231, ext. 31. Mary L. Woods, Geology
Libn.
Staff: 1 full time.
Size: 30,000 maps; 200 atlases; 1 globe; 2,400 aerial photographs.
Annual accessions: 3,000 maps.
Area specializations: North Dakota; United States.
Subject specialization: geology.
Depository for: USGS (topo, geol); Canada; exchange agreements with other state
and some foreign geological surveys.
Serves: University; public.
Interlibrary loan: not available.
Reproduction facility: Xerox.

Valley City

396 VALLEY CITY STATE COLLEGE, DEPARTMENT OF GEOGRA-
PHY*. (58072).
Depository for: TOPOCOM.

OHIO

Akron

397 UNIVERSITY OF AKRON, LIBRARY. (44304) Tel. 216/762-2241. Mrs. Ruth Clinefelter, Social Science Libn.
Size: 1,278 maps; 155 atlases; 20 relief models; 10 gazetteers.
Depository for: USGS (geol—selective).
Serves: University; public.
Interlibrary loan: available.
Reproduction facility: Xerox.

Athens

398 OHIO UNIVERSITY, MAP LIBRARY, Porter Hall. (45701) Tel. 614/594-5571. Dr. Myron T. Sturgeon, Chairman, Geography Department.
Staff: 4 part time.
Size: maps not reported; 65 atlases; 100 relief models; 200 aerial photographs; 33 gazetteers.
Subject specializations: topography; geology.
Depository for: TOPOCOM; USGS (topo, geol).
Serves: University; public.
Interlibrary loan: available.

Bowling Green

399 BOWLING GREEN UNIVERSITY, DEPARTMENT OF GEOGRAPHY, MAP DEPOSITORY. (43402) Tel. 419/353-8411, ext. 3945. Mrs. Joan W. Mancell, Map Libn.
Staff: 1 part time.
Size: 30,000 maps; 150 atlases; 6 globes; 2,000 aerial photographs; 2 gazetteers.
Annual accessions: 2,000 maps; 15 atlases.
Area specializations: Europe; Anglo-America.
Depository for: TOPOCOM.
Serves: University; public.
Interlibrary loan: not available.

Canton

400 CANTON PUBLIC LIBRARY, REFERENCE DIVISION. (44702) Tel. 216/453-9138, ext. 21. Miss Elizabeth Fogle, Division Head.
Size: 3,000 maps; 50 atlases; 3 gazetteers.
Area specializations: Canton; Stark County; Ohio.
Subject specializations: history; topography.
Serves: public.
Interlibrary loan: available.
Reproduction facility: Xerox.

Cincinnati

401 CINCINNATI HISTORICAL SOCIETY, Eden Park. (45202) Tel. 513/241-4622. Lee Jordan, Libn.
Size: 850 maps; 150 atlases.
Area specializations: southwestern Ohio; Cincinnati; Hamilton County.
Serves: public.
Interlibrary loan: not available.
Reproduction facility: photocopy.

402 PUBLIC LIBRARY OF CINCINNATI AND HAMILTON COUNTY, Eighth and Vine Streets. (45202) Tel. 513/241-2636, ext. 13. Rosemary Martin, Map Libn.
Staff: 1 full time; 1 part time.
Size: 97,024 maps; 530 atlases; 4 globes; 12 relief models; 125 aerial photographs.
Area specializations: Cincinnati; Hamilton County; Ohio.
Depository for: TOPOCOM; USGS (topo, geol).
Serves: public.
Interlibrary loan: not available.
Reproduction facility: Xerox.

403 UNIVERSITY OF CINCINNATI, LIBRARY, GEOLOGY-GEOGRA-PHY LIBRARY, 3 Old Tech Building. (45221) Tel. 513/475-4332.
Size: 80,000 maps.
Subject specializations: geology; topography.
Depository for: TOPOCOM; USGS (topo, geol).
Serves: University; public.
Interlibrary loan: not available.
Reproduction facility: Xerox.

Cleveland

404 CASE WESTERN RESERVE UNIVERSITY, GEOLOGY LIBRARY, MAP ROOM, Smith Building. (44106) Tel. 216/368-3762. Miss Flora Lee Rhodes, Libn.
Staff: 1 full time; 1 part time.
Size: 30,000 maps; 800 atlases; 1 globe; 30 relief models.
Annual accessions: 1,000 maps.
Area specialization: United States.
Subject specializations: topography; geology.
Depository for: USGS (topo, geol).
Serves: University; public.
Interlibrary loan: available.
Reproduction facility: Xerox.

405 CLEVELAND PUBLIC LIBRARY, 325 Superior Avenue. (44114) Tel. 216/241-1020, ext. 253. Miss Ethel L. Robinson, Head, General Reference Department.
Staff: 1 part time.
Size: 58,482 maps; 723 atlases; 4 globes; 7 relief models; 172 gazetteers.
Annual accessions: 400 maps; 6 atlases; 15 gazetteers.
Area specializations: Cleveland; Ohio counties.
Subject specializations: history; topography.
Depository for: TOPOCOM; USGS (topo).
Serves: public.
Interlibrary loan: not available.
Reproduction facilities: photocopy; microfilm.

406 DIAMOND SHAMROCK CHEMICAL COMPANY, CENTRAL ENGI-NEERING LIBRARY, 300 Union Commerce Building. (44115) Tel. 216/621-6100. Mrs. Marion B. Tomazic, Libn.
Staff: 1 part time.
Size: not reported.
Subject specialization: geology.

Serves: employees.
Interlibrary loan: available.
Reproduction facilities: photocopy; Xerox.

407 WESTERN RESERVE HISTORICAL SOCIETY, LIBRARY, 10825 East Boulevard. (44106) Tel. 216//721-5722. Kermit J. Pike, Head Libn.
Size: 8,300 maps; 400 atlases; 500 aerial photographs.
Area specializations: Cleveland; Western Reserve; Old Northwest Territory; New England; North America.
Subject specializations: Civil War, particularly battlefields and campaigns; land ownership and land distribution within the Western Reserve.
Serves: students; qualified researchers.
Interlibrary loan: not available.
Reproduction facility: Xerox.

Columbus

408 OHIO HISTORICAL SOCIETY, LIBRARY, 1813 North High Street. (43210) Tel. 614/299-1170. Mrs. Elizabeth R. Martin, Libn.
Size: 2,100 maps; 350 atlases; 2 globes; 20 gazetteers.
Area specializations: Ohio; North America.
Subject specialization: history.
Serves: public.
Interlibrary loan: not available.
Reproduction facilities: photocopy; Xerox; microfilm.

409 OHIO STATE UNIVERSITY, MAP LIBRARY, Room 228, Main Library. 1858 Neil Avenue. (43210) Tel. 614/293-2393. George Schoyer, Libn.
Staff: 1 full time; 2 part time.
Size: 74,631 maps; 250 atlases; 1 globe; 2 gazetteers.
Annual accessions: 1,170 maps; 15 atlases.
Area specializations: Ohio; United States.
Subject specializations: topography; history; economic geography.
Depository for: TOPOCOM; USGS (topo); Canada.
Serves: University; public.
Interlibrary loan: available.
Reproduction facilities: photocopy; Xerox.

410 OHIO STATE UNIVERSITY, ORTON MEMORIAL LIBRARY OF GEOLOGY, 155 S. Oval Drive. (43210) Tel 614/293-2428. Ronald W. Force, Acting Libn.
Staff: 2 part time.
Size: 27,000 maps; 65 atlases.
Annual accessions: 1,500 maps; 5 atlases.
Subject specializations: geology; geodesy; topography.
Depository for: USGS (topo, geol).
Serves: University.
Interlibrary loan: not available.
Reproduction facilities: photocopy; Xerox; microfilm.
Publication: Orton Library Notes. (quarterly)

411 STATE LIBRARY OF OHIO, 65 South Front Street. (43215) Tel. 614/469-2693. Edith Woodward, Documents Libn.
Size: 30,000 maps; 256 atlases.
Annual accessions: 2,400 maps.
Area specialization: Ohio counties.

Subject specialization: topography.
Depository for: USGS (topo).
Serves: public.
Interlibrary loan: not available.
Reproduction facility: photocopy.

Dayton

412   DAYTON AND MONTGOMERY COUNTY PUBLIC LIBRARY*, 215 East Third Street. (45402) Tel. 513/224-1651.
Depository for: TOPOCOM.

Granville

413   DENISON UNIVERSITY, GEOLOGY AND GEOGRAPHY DEPARTMENT. (43023) Tel. 614/582-9181, ext. 347.
Size: not reported.
Depository for: USGS (topo, geol).

Hudson

414   HUDSON LIBRARY AND HISTORICAL SOCIETY, 22 Aurora Street. (44236) Tel. (216/653-6658. Mrs. Theodore S. Sprague, Archivist.
Staff: 1 part time.
Size: 20 maps; 4 atlases; 1 globe; 6 aerial photographs; 7 gazetteers.
Area specializations: Ohio; Western Reserve counties.
Subject specialization: history.
Special cartographic collections: maps and gazetteers dating from 1808–1900; collection of early city directories of Cleveland, Akron, Cincinnati, and Hudson, Ohio.
Serves: public.
Interlibrary loan: not available.
Reproduction facility: photocopy.

Kent

415   KENT STATE UNIVERSITY, MAP LIBRARY. (44240) Tel. 216/672-2243. W. David Voorhees, Map Libn.
Staff: 1 full time; 4 part time.
Size: 100,000 maps; 150 atlases; 30 relief models; 30 gazetteers.
Annual accessions: 10,000 maps; 25 atlases; 200 aerial photographs; 10 gazetteers.
Area specialization: Ohio.
Subject specialization: urban geography.
Depository for: TOPOCOM; USGS (topo).
Serves: University; public.
Interlibrary loan: available.
Reproduction facility: Xerox.

Oxford

416   MIAMI UNIVERSITY, GEOLOGY AND GEOGRAPHY MAP LIBRARY, Shideler Hall. (45056) Tel. 513/523-3216. Dr. A. Dwight Baldwin, Jr.
Staff: 1 full time.
Size: not reported.
Subject specialization: geology.

Depository for: TOPOCOM.
Serves: University; public.
Interlibrary loan: available.
Reproduction facility: Xerox.

Springfield

417　WITTENBERG UNIVERSITY, LIBRARY. (45501) Tel. 513/327-7511. Luella S. Eutsler, Reference Libn.
Size: maps not reported; 100 atlases; 3 globes.
Area specialization: Ohio.
Subject specialization: geology.
Depository for: USGS (topo, geol—Ohio).
Serves: University; public.
Interlibrary loan: available.
Reproduction facility: Xerox.

Toledo

418　TOLEDO PUBLIC LIBRARY, 325 Michigan Street. (43602).
Staff: 2 part time.
Size: 20,000 maps; 3 globes.
Area specializations: Toledo; Ohio.
Subject specialization: local history.
Depository for: USGS (topo, geol).
Serves: public.
Interlibrary loan: not available.
Reproduction facilities: photocopy; microfilm.

419　UNIVERSITY OF TOLEDO, LIBRARY. (43606) Tel. 419/531-5711 ext. 324. William Dale Ebersole, Jr., Assistant Reference Libn.
Staff: 2 part time.
Size: 47,731 maps; 76 atlases; 2 globes; 8 relief models; 33 gazetteers.
Area specialization: Far East.
Subject specializations: topography; geology.
Depository for: TOPOCOM; USGS (topo, geol).
Serves: University; public.
Interlibrary loan: available.
Reproduction facility: photocopy.

Yellow Springs

420　ANTIOCH COLLEGE, LIBRARY*. (45387) Tel. 513/767-7331.
Depository for: TOPOCOM.

OKLAHOMA

Lawton

421　MUSEUM OF THE GREAT PLAINS, P.O. Box 1122. (73501) Tel. 405/ 353-5675. Miss Violet Lee.
Staff: 1 full time.
Size: 8,000 maps; 20 atlases; 150 aerial photographs; 5 gazetteers.
Annual accessions: 500 maps; 2 atlases.
Area specialization: Great Plains of North America.

Subject specialization: topography; geology; soils.
Depository for: USGS (topo, geol); Soil Conservation Service.
Serves: public.
Interlibrary loan: available.
Reproduction facility: photocopy.

Norman

422 UNIVERSITY OF OKLAHOMA, LIBRARY, MAP COLLECTION, Room 407, 401 West Brooks. (73069) Tel. 405/325-3141. Miss Opal Carr, Libn.
Staff: 1 part time.
Size: 67,435 maps; 16,435 aerial photographs.
Area specializations: Oklahoma counties.
Depository for: TOPOCOM.
Serves: University.
Interlibrary loan: not available.
Reproduction facilities: Xerox; microfilm.

Oklahoma City

423 OKLAHOMA COUNTY LIBRARIES, CENTRAL LIBRARY, BUSINESS AND SCIENCE INFORMATION DEPARTMENT, 131 N.W. Third. (73102) Tel. 405/CE 5-0574, ext. 37 or 40. D.R. Babcock, Assistant Libn.
Staff: 1 part time.
Size: 16,000 maps.
Annual accessions: 1,500 maps.
Area specialization: United States.
Subject specializations: topography; geology; mineral resources.
Depository for: USGS (topo, geol); USC&GS.
Interlibrary loan: available.
Reproduction facility: Xerox.

424 OKLAHOMA (STATE) DEPARTMENT OF LIBRARIES*, 109 State Capitol. (73105) Tel. 405/JA 1-3651.
Depository for: TOPOCOM.

Stillwater

425 OKLAHOMA STATE UNIVERSITY, LIBRARY, REFERENCE DEPARTMENT. (74074) Tel. 405/372-6211, ext. 6070. Mrs. D. Corinne Colpitts, Assistant Libn.
Staff: 3 part time.
Size: 70,000 maps; 53 atlases; 4 globes; 10 relief models; 6,600 aerial photographs; 10 gazetteers.
Area specializations: Oklahoma; United States.
Subject specializations: oil and gas investigation maps of the United States; history; Indian territory maps; geology.
Depository for: TOPOCOM; USGS (topo, geol).
Serves: University; public.
Interlibrary loan: not available.
Reproduction facility: Xerox.

Tulsa

426 GILCREASE INSTITUTE, 2500 West Newton. (74106) Tel. 918/584-2351, ext. 298. G.P. Edwards, Curator.
Staff: 2 full time.
Size: 301 maps.
Area specializations: Oklahoma; trans-Mississippi West.
Subject specializations: discovery and exploration; settlement.
Serves: public.
Interlibrary loan: not available.
Reproduction facility: photocopy.

427 TULSA CITY–COUNTY LIBRARY, BUSINESS AND TECHNOLOGY DEPARTMENT, 400 Civic Center. (74103) Tel. 918/582-8831, ext. 213. Donna Lemon.
Staff: 6 full time.
Size: 60,000 maps.
Annual accessions: 1,600 maps.
Subject specializations: geology; topography.
Special cartographic collections: U.S. Land Office plat maps—19 states; A. I. Levorsen Collection of geology maps.
Depository for: USGS (topo, geol).
Serves: public.
Interlibrary loan: not available.
Reproduction facility: Xerox.

428 UNIVERSITY OF TULSA, LIBRARY*, Seventh and College Avenue. (74104) Tel. 918/WE 9-6351, ext. 351.
Depository for: TOPOCOM.

OREGON

Bend

429 CENTRAL OREGON COMMUNITY COLLEGE. (97701) Tel. 503/382-6112, ext. 81. Ed Jackson, Assistant Libn.
Size: maps not reported; 10 atlases; 1 globe; 2 relief models; 6 gazetteers.
Special cartographic collections: U.S. Forest Service maps; USGS geologic maps (housed in Geology Department).
Depository for: USGS (geol).
Serves: College; public.
Interlibrary loan: available.
Reproduction facilities: Xerox; microfilm.

Corvallis

430 OREGON STATE UNIVERSITY, LIBRARY. (97331) Tel. 503/754-2971. Mrs. Etta Judd, Libn.
Staff: 1 full time; 2 part time.
Size: 68,925 maps; 200 atlases; 2 globes; 26 relief models; 18,350 aerial photographs; 143 gazetteers.
Annual accessions: 2,500 maps; 10 atlases; 750 aerial photographs.
Area specializations: Oregon; United States.
Subject specializations: geology; topography.
Depository for: TOPOCOM; USGS (topo, geol).

Serves: University; public.
Interlibrary loan: available.
Reproduction facility: Xerox.
Publication: selected acquisitions listed in the Library's *New Book List.*

Eugene

431 UNIVERSITY OF OREGON, MAP LIBRARY, 165 Condon Hall. (97403) Tel. 503/342-1411, ext. 1350. Rebecca A. Wilson, Map Libn.
Staff: 1 full time; 5 part time.
Size: 91,000 maps; 200 atlases; 170 relief models; 40,000 aerial photographs; 40 gazetteers.
Area specializations: Oregon; Latin America.
Depository for: TOPOCOM; USGS (topo, geol).
Serves: University; public.
Interlibrary loan: not available.
Reproduction facilities: Xerox; microfilm.

Portland

432 LIBRARY ASSOCIATION OF PORTLAND, 801 S.W. 10th Avenue. (97205) Tel. 503/223-7201. Clyde Marshall, Reference Libn.
Staff: 2 part time.
Size: 40,033 maps; 500 atlases; 17 relief models; 200 gazetteers.
Annual accessions: 2,000 maps.
Area specializations: Oregon; Pacific Northwest.
Subject specializations: topography; geology; political geography; transportation.
Depository for: TOPOCOM; USGS (topo).
Serves: public.
Interlibrary loan: not available.
Reproduction facility: Denison copier.

433 OREGON HISTORICAL SOCIETY, 1230 S.W. Park Avenue. (97205) Tel. 503/222-1741, ext. 51. Robert E. Fessenden, Chief Libn.
Size: 5,000 maps; 100 atlases; 1 globe; 1 relief model; 25 gazetteers.
Annual accessions: 100 maps.
Area specializations: Pacific Northwest; Oregon; North Pacific Basin.
Special cartographic collections: Carey Collection of 17th to 19th century engraved maps of Oregon; photostats of Northwest coastal charts from French and Spanish Archives; manuscript maps of Oregon; U.S. Coast Survey charts, 1878–1900.
Depository for: USGS (topo—Oregon); Oregon State Highway Department.
Serves: public.
Interlibrary loan: not available.
Reproduction facilities: photocopy; Xerox; microfilm.

434 PORTLAND STATE COLLEGE, LIBRARY, P.O. Box 1151. (97207) Tel. 503/226-7271, ext. 493. Mrs. Annette Bartholomae, Social Science Libn.
Staff: 1 part time.
Size: 17,827 maps; 185 atlases; 1 globe; 2 relief models; 36 aerial photographs; 45 gazetteers.
Annual accessions: 2,591 maps.
Depository for: TOPOCOM.
Serves: College; public.
Interlibrary loan: not available.
Reproduction facility: Xerox.

Salem

435 OREGON STATE LIBRARY, State Library Building. (97310) Tel. 503/ 364-2171, ext. 304.
Size: 16,150 maps; 150 atlases; 1 globe; 35 relief models; 20 gazetteers.
Area specialization: Oregon.
Subject specialization: topography.
Depository for: TOPOCOM; USGS (topo).
Serves: public.
Interlibrary loan: available.
Reproduction facilities: photocopy; Xerox.

PENNSYLVANIA

Bethlehem

436 LEHIGH UNIVERSITY, LIBRARY. (18015) Tel. 215/867-5071, ext. 241. Miss Margaret Dennis, Assistant Libn.
Staff: 1 part time.
Size: not reported.
Area specializations: Pennsylvania; Canada; Amazon Valley.
Subject specializations: local history; geology; topography.
Depository for: USGS (topo, geol).
Serves: University; public.
Interlibrary loan: available.
Reproduction facility: Xerox.

437 MORAVIAN COLLEGE, EARTH SCIENCES DEPARTMENT*. (18018) Dr. Richard E. Myers.
Depository for: TOPOCOM.

Bryn Mawr

438 BRYN MAWR COLLEGE, LIBRARY*. (19010) Tel. 215/LA 5-1000.
Depository for: TOPOCOM.

Carlisle Barracks

439 U.S. ARMY WAR COLLEGE, LIBRARY, MAP SECTION. (17013) Tel. 717/245-4061. Richard L. Weary. Map Libn.
Staff: 1 part time.
Size: 33,923 maps; 25 atlases; 1 globe; 250 relief models; 100 gazetteers.
Annual accessions: 1,973 maps; 3 atlases.
Subject specialization: political geography.
Serves: College.
Interlibrary loan: not available.

Gettysburg

440 GETTYSBURG COLLEGE, LIBRARY, AUDIO-VISUAL DEPART-MENT. (17325) Tel. 717/334-3131, ext. 295. Doris M. Kemler, Audio-Visual Libn.
Staff: 2 part time.
Size: 897 maps; 15 atlases; 1 globe; 3 gazetteers.
Annual accessions: 25 maps.

Area specializations: Europe; North America; South America.
Subject specialization: European history.
Special cartographic collection: Stuckenberg Collection of 588 16th to 18th century rare maps of Europe.
Serves: College.
Interlibrary loan: available (restricted).

Harrisburg

441　PENNSYLVANIA (STATE) BUREAU OF LAND RECORDS, Room 543, "E" Floor, North Wing, Main Capitol Building. (17120) Tel. 717/787-6779. Blair A. Griffith, Director.
Staff: 4 full time.
Size: 443 maps.
Annual accessions: 12 maps.
Area specializations: Pennsylvania counties.
Subject specializations: original land grants from the Penns and the Commonwealth of Pennsylvania.
Depository for: Commonwealth of Pennsylvania.
Serves: public.
Interlibrary loan: available.
Reproduction facility: Diazo.

442　PENNSYLVANIA (STATE) GEOLOGIC SURVEY, LIBRARY, Old Museum Building. (17120) Tel. 717/787-5828. Miss Judith Herring.
Staff: 1 full time.
Size: 45,000 maps; 10,000 aerial photographs.
Annual accessions: 1,500 maps; 1,500 aerial photographs.
Area specialization: Pennsylvania.
Subject specialization: geology; topography.
Depository for: USGS (topo, geol).
Serves: public.
Interlibrary loan: available.
Reproduction facilities: Xerox; Ozalid.

443　PENNSYLVANIA (STATE) HISTORICAL AND MUSEUM COMMISSION, BUREAU OF ARCHIVES AND HISTORY, William Penn Memorial and Archives Building, Box 1026. (17108) Tel. 717/787-2701 and 2761. William H. Work, State Archivist; Mrs. Betsey Smith, Reference Libn.
Size: 1,833 maps; 53 atlases; 27 cartons of aerial photographs.
Area specialization: Pennsylvania.
Subject specializations: roads; canals; history.
Special cartographic collections: State road and turnpike maps, 1706–1873; aerial photographic survey, 1938–1940; 53 map books of Canal Commissioners' Maps, 1810–1881.
Depository for: USGS (topo—Pennsylvania).
Serves: students; qualified researchers.
Interlibrary loan: not available.
Reproduction facilities: photocopy; Xerox; microfilm.
Publication: Inventory of Canal Commissioners' Maps. 1968.

444　PENNSYLVANIA STATE LIBRARY, GENERAL LIBRARY BUREAU, Box 1601. (17126) Tel. 717/787-3942. A. Hunter Rineer, Jr., Director.
Staff: 1 part time.
Size: not reported.
Area specialization: Pennsylvania.

Subject specialization: local history.
Depository for: USGS (topo).
Serves: employees; public.
Interlibrary loan: not available.
Reproduction facility: photocopy.

Indiana

445 INDIANA UNIVERSITY OF PENNSYLVANIA, GEOGRAPHY DE-
PARTMENT, MAP LIBRARY. (15701) Tel. 412/463-9111, ext. 246. James
E. Payne, Associate Professor of Geography.
Staff: 2 part time.
Size: 1,200 maps; 50 atlases; 75 relief models; 3,000 aerial photographs.
Subject specializations: economic geography; urban geography.
Serves: University.
Interlibrary loan: not available.

Kutztown

446 KUTZTOWN STATE COLLEGE, ROHRBACH LIBRARY. (19530) Tel.
215/683-3511, ext. 224. Mrs. Anita T. Sprankle, Libn.
Staff: 1 part time.
Size: 1,300 maps; 70 atlases; 3 globes; 2 relief models; 2 gazetteers.
Annual accessions: 250 maps; 3 atlases.
Area specializations: Pennsylvania; United States.
Subject specializations: topography; city planning.
Serves: College.
Interlibrary loan: not available.
Reproduction facility: photocopy.

Lancaster

447 LANCASTER MENNONITE CONFERENCE, HISTORICAL SOCIETY
LIBRARY AND ARCHIVES, 2215 Mill Stream Road. (17602) Tel. 717/
393-9745. Ira D. Landis, Archivist and Genealogist.
Staff: 2 full time; 2 part time.
Size: 75 maps; 42 atlases.
Area specializations: Lancaster County; southeastern Pennsylvania.
Subject specializations: history; genealogy.
Serves: public.
Interlibrary loan: not available.
Reproduction facility: photocopy.

Lewisburg

448 BUCKNELL UNIVERSITY, ELLEN CLARKE BERTRAND LIBRARY.
(17837) Tel. 717/524-3056. Mrs. Zoia Horn, Head Reference Department.
Size: 6,061 maps; 816 atlases; 1 globe.
Depository for: TOPOCOM.
Serves: University; public.
Interlibrary loan: available.
Reproduction facility: Xerox.

Meadville

449 CRAWFORD COUNTY HISTORICAL SOCIETY, 848 North Main Street. (16335) Tel. 814/333-8131. Halver W. Getchell, Secretary.
Staff: 1 part time.
Size: 300 maps; 10 atlases; 2 globes; 2 gazetteers.
Area specializations: Meadville; Crawford county; northwestern Pennsylvania.
Subject specializations: history; transportation; land surveys.
Special cartographic collection: Pennsylvania Donation Land and Holland Land Company tract surveys and early assignments.
Serves: public.
Interlibrary loan: not available.
Reproduction facility: photocopy.

Millersville

450 MILLERSVILLE STATE COLLEGE, GEOGRAPHY DEPARTMENT, MAP COLLECTION. (17551) Tel. 717/872-5411, ext. 251. Arthur C. Lord, Acting Map Libn.
Staff: 2 part time.
Size: 30,000 maps; 20 atlases; 9 globes; 25 relief models; 500 aerial photographs; 2 gazetteers.
Annual accessions: 500 maps; 2 atlases; 100 aerial photographs.
Area specializations: Middle Atlantic States.
Subject specialization: topography.
Depository for: TOPOCOM; USGS (topo—selective).
Serves: College; public.
Interlibrary loan: not available.
Reproduction facilities: photocopy; Xerox.

Philadelphia

451 CITY PLANNING COMMISSION, 14th Floor, City Hall Annex. (19107) Tel. 215/686-4622. Alois K. Strobl, Chief Cartographer.
Staff: 1 full time.
Size: not reported.
Area specialization: Philadelphia.
Subject specializations: land use; demography.
Serves: employees.
Interlibrary loan: not available.

452 FREE LIBRARY OF PHILADELPHIA, SOCIAL SCIENCE AND HISTORY DEPARTMENT, MAP COLLECTION, Logan Square. (19103) Tel. 215/MU 6-5397. Jeremiah Post, Librarian-in-Charge.
Staff: 2 full time.
Size: 116,000 maps; 2,700 atlases; 15 globes; 14 relief models; 500 aerial photographs; 800 gazetteers.
Annual accessions: 2,000 maps; 30 atlases; 20 gazetteers.
Area specializations: Philadelphia; Pennsylvania; northeastern and Middle Atlantic States.
Subject specializations: cartography; history; geography; travel guides.
Special cartographic collections: William G. Kelso Collection of Jansson-Visscher maps of America; fire insurance atlases of Philadelphia.
Depository for: TOPOCOM; USGS (topo, geol).
Serves: public.

Interlibrary loan: not available.
Reproduction facilities: photocopy; Xerox; microfilm.
Publication: The Map collection, 1969 (a brochure).

453 HISTORICAL SOCIETY OF PENNSYLVANIA, 1300 Locust Street. (19107) Tel. 215/PE 5-2121. Conrad Wilson, Chief of Manuscripts.
Staff: 4 part time.
Size: 4,300 maps; 450 atlases.
Area specializations: Philadelphia; Pennsylvania.
Subject specialization: history.
Serves: public.
Interlibrary loan: not available.
Reproduction facilities: photocopy; Xerox; microfilm.

454 LIBRARY COMPANY OF PHILADELPHIA, 1314 Locust Street. (19107) Tel. 215/KI 6-3181. Edwin Wolf, Libn.
Size: not reported.
Special cartographic collection: American maps dating from the late 1500's to the 1800's.
Serves: public.
Interlibrary loan: not available.
Reproduction facilities: photocopy; Xerox; microfilm.

Pittsburgh

455 CARNEGIE LIBRARY OF PITTSBURGH, 4400 Forbes Avenue. (15213) Tel. 412/621-7300, ext. 232. Virginia L. Garland, Science and Technology Department Libn.
Size: 3,000 maps; 200 atlases; 1 globe.
Area specializations: Pittsburgh; Pennsylvania.
Subject specializations: soil surveys; topography; geology.
Depository for: USGS (topo, geol).
Serves: public.
Interlibrary loan: not available.
Reproduction facilities: photocopy; Xerox.

456 HISTORICAL SOCIETY OF WESTERN PENNSYLVANIA, LIBRARY, 4338 Bigelow Boulevard. (15213) Tel. 412/681-7000. Ruth K. Salisbury, Libn.
Size: 235 maps; 40 atlases.
Area specializations: Pittsburgh; western Pennsylvania.
Serves: public.
Interlibrary loan: not available.

457 UNIVERSITY OF PITTSBURGH, DARLINGTON MEMORIAL LIBRARY, 601 Cathedral of Learning. (15213) Tel. 412/621-3500, ext. 234. G. M. Jones, Libn.
Staff: 2 full time.
Size: 710 maps; 60 atlases; 2 gazetteers.
Area specializations: western Pennsylvania; United States.
Subject specializations: colonial history; local history.
Serves: University; public.
Interlibrary loan: not available.
Reproduction facility: Xerox.

458 UNIVERSITY OF PITTSBURGH, HILLMAN LIBRARY, DOCU-
MENTS/MAP OFFICE, G-8. (15213) Tel. 412/621-3500, ext. 7288. M.B.
Miller, Libn.
Staff: 2 part time.
Size: 51,204 maps.
Annual accessions: 1,000 maps.
Depository for: TOPOCOM; USGS (topo).
Serves: University; public.
Interlibrary loan: not available.
Reproduction facility: Xerox.

Slippery Rock

459 SLIPPERY ROCK STATE COLLEGE, DEPARTMENT OF GEOGRA-
PHY*. (16057).
Depository for: TOPOCOM.

Swarthmore

460 SWARTHMORE COLLEGE, LIBRARY. (19081) Tel. 215/KI 3-0200, ext.
431. Howard H. Williams, Reference Libn.
Size: 12,141 maps; 154 atlases; 3 globes; 11 gazetteers.
Annual accessions: 160 maps; 4 atlases.
Area specializations: Pennsylvania; Delaware; Maryland.
Subject specializations: geology; Quaker history.
Special cartographic collection: British Ordnance Survey maps.
Depository for: USGS (geol—eastern United States).
Serves: College; public (by permission).
Interlibrary loan: available.
Reproduction facility: Xerox.

University Park

461 PENNSYLVANIA STATE UNIVERSITY, PATTEE LIBRARY. (16802)
Tel. 814/865-6368. Mrs. Ruby M. Miller, Assistant Reference Libn.
Staff: 2 full time; 2 part time.
Size: 126,000 maps; 1,000 atlases; 3 globes; 200 gazetteers.
Annual accessions: 7,500 maps.
Area specializations: Pennsylvania; western and central Europe; USSR; United
States; Canada; Africa.
Subject specializations: city planning; topography; transportation; agriculture;
geology; demography.
Depository for: TOPOCOM; USGS (topo, geol); Canada; USC&GS.
Serves: University; public.
Interlibrary loan: not available.
Reproduction facilities: photocopy; Xerox; Denison copier.

PUERTO RICO

Rio Piedras

462 UNIVERSITY OF PUERTO RICO, GENERAL LIBRARY, DOCU-
MENTS AND MAPS ROOM. (00931) Josefa J. Howard, Libn.
Staff: 1 part time.
Size: 24,130 maps; 55 atlases; 2 globes.

Subject specializations: topography; geology.
Depository for: TOPOCOM; USGS (topo, geol).
Serves: University; public.
Interlibrary loan: not available.
Reproduction facility: photocopy.

RHODE ISLAND

Kingston

463 UNIVERSITY OF RHODE ISLAND, LIBRARY*. (02881) Tel. 401/792-2666.
Depository for: TOPOCOM.

Newport

464 NEWPORT HISTORICAL SOCIETY, 82 Touro Street. (02840) Tel. 401/846-0813.
Size: 275 maps; 20 atlases.
Area specializations: Newport; Rhode Island.
Subject specialization: history.
Serves: public.
Interlibrary loan: not available.

Providence

465 BROWN UNIVERSITY, JOHN CARTER BROWN LIBRARY. (02912) Tel. 401/863-2725. Jeannette D. Black, Curator of Maps.
Staff: 1 full time.
Size: 10,000 maps; 50 gazetteers.
Area specialization: Western Hemisphere.
Subject specializations: Colonial maps; hydrography; historical geography.
Special cartographic collections: 16th century Italian maps of the Americas; maritime charts of the Atlantic and Pacific Oceans.
Serves: University; public.
Interlibrary loan: not available.
Reproduction facility: photocopy.

466 BROWN UNIVERSITY, LIBRARY. (02912) Tel. 401/863-2517. Dorothy Day, Social Studies Libn.
Staff: 4 part time.
Size: 52,270 maps; 350 atlases; 1 globe; 10 relief models; 135 gazetteers.
Annual accessions: 2,000 maps.
Depository for: TOPOCOM; USGS (geol).
Serves: University.
Interlibrary loan: not available.
Reproduction facilities: photocopy; Xerox; microfilm.

467 RHODE ISLAND HISTORICAL SOCIETY, LIBRARY, 121 Hope Street. (02906) Tel. 401/331-8575. Albert T. Klyberg, Libn.
Size: 2,000 maps; 50 atlases.
Annual accessions: 50 maps.
Area specializations: Rhode Island; New England.

Serves: public.
Interlibrary loan: not available.
Reproduction facilities: photocopy; Xerox; microfilm.

SOUTH CAROLINA

Clemson

468 CLEMSON UNIVERSITY, LIBRARY*. (29631) Tel. 803/654-2421, ext. 260.
Depository for: TOPOCOM.

Columbia

469 SOUTH CAROLINA (STATE) DEPARTMENT OF ARCHIVES AND HISTORY, P.O. Box 11188, Capitol Station. (29211) Tel. 803/758-3438. Miss Ruth S. Green, Inventory Archivist.
Size: 1,621 maps; 5 atlases.
Area specializations: South Carolina; southeastern United States.
Subject specializations: discovery and exploration; field surveys.
Special cartographic collections: survey maps—state, county, township, and city boundaries; canal, river, road and railroad surveys.
Serves: public.
Interlibrary loan: not available.
Reproduction facility: photocopy.

470 UNIVERSITY OF SOUTH CAROLINA, McKISSICK MEMORIAL LIBRARY. (29208) Tel. 803/777-3142. Mrs. Davy Jo Ridge, Reference Libn.
Size: 20,000 maps; 102 atlases; 1 globe; 25 gazetteers.
Depository for: TOPOCOM; USGS (topo, geol).
Serves: University; public.
Interlibrary loan: not available.
Reproduction facility: Xerox.

471 UNIVERSITY OF SOUTH CAROLINA, SOUTH CAROLINIANA LIBRARY. (29208) Tel. 803/777-3131. E. L. Inabinett, Libn.
Size: 1,742 maps.
Area specializations: South Carolina; southeastern United States.
Subject specialization: local history.
Serves: University; public.
Interlibrary loan: not available.
Reproduction facilities: photocopy; Xerox; microfilm.

Greenville

472 FURMAN UNIVERSITY, DEPARTMENT OF GEOLOGY. (29613) Tel. 803/246-3550, ext. 340. Van Price, Acting Department Chairman.
Staff: 2 part time.
Size: not reported.
Depository for: USGS (topo).
Serves: University; public.
Reproduction facility: Xerox.

SOUTH DAKOTA

Pierre

473 SOUTH DAKOTA STATE HISTORICAL SOCIETY, Soldier's Memorial Building. (57501) Tel. 605/224-3293. Miss Janice Fleming, Libn.
Size: 500 maps; 200 atlases.
Area specializations: South Dakota; trans-Mississippi West.
Subject specializations: railroads; roads; trails.
Serves: public.
Interlibrary loan: not available.
Reproduction facility: microfilm.

Rapid City

474 SOUTH DAKOTA SCHOOL OF MINES AND TECHNOLOGY, LIBRARY. (57701) Tel. 605/349-2418. Estella Helgeson, Associate Libn.
Size: maps not reported; 12 atlases; 1 globe.
Area specialization: South Dakota.
Subject specializations: geology; mines and minerals.
Depository for: USGS (topo, geol).
Serves: School; public.
Reproduction facility: Xerox.

Vermillion

475 UNIVERSITY OF SOUTH DAKOTA, I. D. WEEKS LIBRARY. (57069) Tel. 605/677-5371. Virgil F. Massman, Director.
Size: not reported.
Area specialization: upper Missouri Valley.
Special cartographic collection: 147 18th and 19th century maps showing boundary changes, routes of explorers, railroad surveys, and Indian settlements.
Serves: University; public.
Interlibrary loan: not available.
Reproduction facility: photocopy.

TENNESSEE

Chattanooga

476 CHATTANOOGA PUBLIC LIBRARY, 601 McCallie Avenue. (37403) Tel. 615/266-6451, ext. 24. Mrs. Davis Seaborn; Head, Historical Department.
Size: 457 maps; 105 folios; 6 atlases; 3 relief models; 17 aerial photographs.
Area specializations: Chattanooga; Hamilton County; Tennessee; Georgia; North Carolina; Virginia.
Subject specialization: local history.
Serves: public.
Interlibrary loan: not available.
Reproduction facility: photocopy.

477 TENNESSEE VALLEY AUTHORITY, MAPS AND SURVEYS BRANCH, MAP INFORMATION AND RECORDS UNIT, 110 Pound Building. (37401) Tel. 615/755-2125. T. V. Young, Civil Engineer.
Staff: 6 full time; 2 part time.
Size: 625,000 maps; 10 relief models; 250,000 aerial photographs.

Annual accessions: 25,000 maps; 10,000 aerial photographs.
Area specialization: Tennessee Valley region.
Subject specializations: topography; hydrography; navigation; geology; soils; surveys and mapping.
Special cartographic collections: special project and tributary development area maps; aerial photographs.
Depository for: USGS (topo).
Serves: public.
Interlibrary loan: not available.
Reproduction facilities: photocopy; Xerox; microfilm.

Johnson City

478   EAST TENNESSEE STATE UNIVERSITY, MAP LIBRARY. (37601) Tel. 615/926-1112, ext. 282. Mr. Majid Ejlali, Libn.
Staff: 1 full time; 6 part time.
Size: 50,000 maps.
Annual accessions: 1,000 maps.
Area specialization: United States.
Subject specialization: topography.
Depository for: TOPOCOM; USGS (topo, geol).
Serves: University; public.
Interlibrary loan: available.
Reproduction facilities: Xerox; microfilm.

Knoxville

479   TENNESSEE VALLEY AUTHORITY, MAPS AND ENGINEERING RECORDS, 416 Union Avenue. (37902) Tel. 615/522-7181, ext. 2675. Benton McKeehan, Head, Map and Engineering Records.
Staff: 13 full time.
Size: 22,200 maps; 100 atlases; 17 relief models; 2,000 aerial photographs; 50 gazetteers.
Annual accessions: 1,000 maps; 5 atlases; 72 aerial photographs.
Area specializations: Tennessee Valley region; Tennessee River Basin.
Subject specializations: planimetry; topography; water navigation; flood control.
Serves: public (subject to security regulations); also serves as official sales department for TVA maps, charts, and graphics.
Interlibrary loan: not available.
Reproduction facilities: photocopy; Xerox; microfilm; white and blue prints.
Publication: Selected List of Maps and Charts.

480   UNIVERSITY OF TENNESSEE, MAP LIBRARY, Geography and Geology Building. (37916) Tel. 615/974-2418. Dr. Robert G. Long, Acting Head, Department of Geography.
Staff: 2 part time.
Size: 50,000 maps; 40 atlases; 1 relief model; 8 globes; 20 aerial photographs (107 index mosaics).
Annual accessions: 500 maps; 2 atlases.
Area specialization: United States.
Subject specialization: geology.
Depository for: TOPOCOM; USGS (topo, geol).
Serves: University; public.
Interlibrary loan: available.
Reproduction facility: photocopy.

Memphis

481 COSSITT-GOODWYN LIBRARIES, 33 South Front Street. (38103) Tel. 901/526-8431. Tine T. McCann, Libn., Documents Division.

Staff: 2 part time.
Size: 33,000 maps; 125 atlases; 3 globes.
Annual accessions: 2,000 maps; 5 atlases.
Depository for: USGS (topo, geol).
Interlibrary loan: available.
Reproduction facility: Xerox.

482 MEMPHIS STATE UNIVERSITY, MAP LIBRARY*, Room 122, Johnson Hall. (38111).
Depository for: TOPOCOM.

Murfreesboro

483 MIDDLE TENNESSEE STATE UNIVERSITY, DEPARTMENT OF GEOGRAPHY*. (37130).
Depository for: TOPOCOM.

Nashville

484 JOINT UNIVERSITY LIBRARIES, SCIENCE LIBRARY. (37203) Tel. 615/254-5411, ext. 7474.

Size: not reported.
Subject specializations: geology; topography.
Depository for: USGS (topo, geol).
Serves: University; public.
Interlibrary loan: not available.
Reproduction facility: Xerox.

485 TENNESSEE STATE LIBRARY AND ARCHIVES, ARCHIVES AND RECORDS MANAGEMENT SECTION, 403 7th Avenue North. (37219) Tel. 615/741-2561. Mrs. Cleo A. Hughes, Senior Archivist.

Size: 800 maps (does not include depository collection).
Area specialization: Tennessee.
Subject specialization: local history.
Depository for: TOPOCOM; USGS (topo, geol).
Serves: employees; public.
Interlibrary loan: not available.
Reproduction facilities: photocopy; Xerox; microfilm.

TEXAS

Austin

486 TEXAS STATE LIBRARY, ARCHIVES DIVISION, 1201 Brazos Street. (78711) Tel. 512/GR 5-2445. Mrs. Viola Walpole.

Staff: 1 full time.
Size: 2,000 maps.
Area specializations: Texas; southwestern United States.
Serves: public.
Interlibrary loan: not available.
Reproduction facilities: photocopy; Xerox.

Publication: The Map Collection of the Texas State Archives, 1527–1900. James M. Day and Ann B. Dunlap. Austin, Texas Library and Historical Commission, 1962.

487 UNIVERSITY OF TEXAS, DEPARTMENT OF GEOGRAPHY. (78712) Tel. 512/GR 1-5116. Dr. Robert K. Holz, Associate Professor of Geography.
Staff: 2 part time.
Size: 1,500 flat maps; 450 wall maps; 125 atlases; 6 globes; 20 relief models; 7,000 aerial photographs; 5 gazetteers.
Annual accessions: 300 flat maps; 15 wall maps; 300 aerial photographs.
Area specializations: Latin America; east central Europe.
Subject specialization: geomorphology.
Serves: University; public (by permission).
Interlibrary loan: not available.
Reproduction facility: Xerox.

488 UNIVERSITY OF TEXAS, LIBRARY. (78712). Tel. 512/GR 1-7521, 7516, 1257. Dr. Chester A. Kielman (Texas); Mrs. Thelma Guion (Geology); Dr. Nettie Benson (Latin American Collection); Miss Mildred Hildreth (TOPOCOM).
Size: 65,000 maps; 1,250 atlases.
Area specializations: Texas; southwestern United States; Latin America.
Subject specializations: geology; topography.
Depository for: TOPOCOM; USGS (topo, geol).
Serves: University; public.
Interlibrary loan: not available.
Reproduction facilities: photocopy; Xerox; microfilm.
Note: Texas maps are located in the Texas History Center; USGS maps are located in the Geology Library; and TOPOCOM maps are located in the Documents Collection.

Canyon

489 WEST TEXAS STATE UNIVERSITY, LIBRARY*. (79015) Tel. 806/OL 5-7141, ext. 2207.
Depository for: TOPOCOM.

College Station

490 TEXAS A & M UNIVERSITY, LIBRARY. (77843) Tel. 713/845-6111.
Size: 11,084 maps; 515 atlases; 1 globe; 10 aerial photographs.
Annual accessions: 150 maps; 5 atlases.
Subject specialization: geology.
Special cartographic collections: weather maps; oil field maps.
Serves: University; public.
Interlibrary loan: available.
Reproduction facility: Xerox.

Dallas

491 DALLAS PUBLIC LIBRARY, 1954 Commerce. (75201) Tel. 214/RI 8-9071. Mrs. Lucile A. Boykin, Head, Texas History and Genealogy Department.
Size: 236 maps; 6 atlases; 3 aerial photographs.
Area specializations: Dallas; Texas; southwestern United States.

Subject specializations: local history; genealogy.
Serves: public.
Interlibrary loan: not available.
Reproduction facilities: photocopy; microfilm.

492 MOBIL RESEARCH AND DEVELOPMENT CORPORATION, RE-SEARCH DEPARTMENT, FIELD RESEARCH LABORATORY LI-BRARY, 3600 Duncalville Road. (75221) Tel. 214/331-6531, ext. 545. Dudley B. Schoolfield, Cataloger.
Size: 1,200 maps; 33 atlases; 1 globe; 2 gazetteers.
Annual accessions: 40 maps; 4 atlases.
Area specialization: Western Hemisphere.
Subject specializations: geology; mineral resources; topography; oil and gas.
Serves: employees; public (by permission).
Interlibrary loan: not available.
Reproduction facility: Xerox.

493 SOUTHERN METHODIST UNIVERSTIY, SCIENCE ENGINEERING LIBRARY, EDWIN J. FOSCUE MAP LIBRARY. (75222) Tel. 214/EM 3-5611, ext. 480. Mrs. Beverly J. Holmes, Map Libn.
Staff: 2 part time.
Size: 127,200 maps; 150 atlases; 1 globe; 3,550 aerial photographs; 150 gazetteers.
Annual accessions: 3,500 maps; 25 atlases; 10 gazetteers.
Area specializations: Texas; southwestern United States; western Europe; Latin America.
Subject specializations: geology; topography; soils; oil and gas; transportation.
Special cartographic collection: DeGolyer Collection (geology).
Depository for: TOPOCOM; USGS (topo, geol); USDA Soil Surveys; USC&GS (nautical and aeronautical charts).
Serves: University; public.
Interlibrary loan: available.
Reproduction facilities: photocopy; Xerox; microfilm.

Denton

494 NORTH TEXAS STATE UNIVERSITY, LIBRARY. (76203) Tel. 817/387-4511. Mrs. Velma Cathey, Libn.
Size: 2,466 maps; 1 globe.
Annual accessions: 400 maps.
Depository for: USGS (topo—Texas).
Serves: University; public.
Interlibrary loan: available (restricted).
Reproduction facility: Xerox.

El Paso

495 UNIVERSITY OF TEXAS AT EL PASO, LIBRARY*. (79999) Tel. 915/542-5684.
Depository for: TOPOCOM.
Serves: University; public.

Fort Worth

496 FORT WORTH PUBLIC LIBRARY, EARTH SCIENCE LIBRARY, 9th and Throckmorton Streets. (76102) Tel. 817/ED 5-4781, ext. 40 or 22. June Wasserman, Head, Business and Technology Department.
Staff: 1 full time.

Size: 6,747 maps; 4 atlases.
Area specialization: southwestern United States.
Subject specializations: topography; geology; oil and gas.
Depository for: USGS (topo—southwestern United States).
Serves: public.
Interlibrary loan: available.
Reproduction facilities: photocopy; Xerox.

Galveston

497 ROSENBERG LIBRARY, 823 Tremont. (77550) Tel. 713/763-8854, ext. 6. Mrs. Robert Davies, Reference Libn.; Robert C. Park, Archivist.
Staff: 2 part time.
Size: 7,327 maps; 45 atlases; 8 gazetteers. In Archives: 460 maps; 6 atlases.
Area specializations: Galveston; Texas.
Subject specializations: geology; topography.
Depository for: USGS (topo, geol).
Serves: public.
Interlibrary loan: not available.
Reproduction facilities: photocopy; Xerox.

Houston

498 ESSO PRODUCTION RESEARCH LIBRARY, P.O. Box 2189. (77001) Tel. 713/622-4222. Carrie W. Eagon, Chief Libn.
Staff: 1 part time.
Size: 10,000 maps; 50 atlases; 1 globe; 5 gazetteers.
Subject specializations: geology; topography.
Serves: employees.
Interlibrary loan: available.
Reproduction facilities: photocopy; Xerox; microfilm.

499 HOUSTON PUBLIC LIBRARY, 500 McKinney Avenue. (77002) Tel. 713/ CA 4-5441.
Size: 4,429 maps; 127 atlases; 19 gazetteers.
Annual accessions: 400 maps; 10 atlases; 4 gazetteers.
Area specialization: Texas.
Subject specialization: topography.
Serves: public.
Interlibrary loan: not available.
Reproduction facility: Xerox.

500 RICE UNIVERSITY, FONDREN LIBRARY, MAP ROOM M 17, Box 1892. (77001) Tel. 713/528-4141, ext. 819. Georgia A. Frazer, Map Libn.
Staff: 1 full time; 7 part time.
Size: 12,100 maps; 225 atlases; 3 globes; 5 relief models; 44 gazetteers.
Annual accessions: 700 maps; 3 atlases.
Subject specializations: geology; topography; history.
Depository for: TOPOCOM; USGS (topo, geol—selective).
Serves: University; public.
Reproduction facility: Xerox.

501 TENNECO OIL COMPANY, EXPLORATION STUDIES LIBRARY, P.O. Box 2511. (77001) Tel. 713/229-2310. Carolyn W. Nash, Libn.
Staff: 1 full time.
Size: 2,600 maps; 3 atlases; 1 relief model; 2 gazetteers.

Subject specializations: geology; petrology; mineral resources.
Serves: employees; public (by permission).
Interlibrary loan: available.
Reproduction facility: Xerox.

502 UNIVERSITY OF HOUSTON, LIBRARY, Cullen Boulevard. (77004) Tel. 713/748-6600, ext. 356. Miss Sara Aull, Science Libn.
Staff: 2 part time.
Size: 5,192 maps.
Annual accessions: 1,500 maps.
Area specializations: Texas; Arkansas; Colorado; Louisiana; Oklahoma; New Mexico.
Subject specialization: geology.
Depository for: USGS (topo—southwestern United States, geol).
Serves: University; public.
Interlibrary loan: not available.
Reproduction facilities: Xerox; microfilm.

Midland

503 MIDLAND COUNTY LIBRARY, TECHNICAL DEPARTMENT, P.O. Box 1191. (79701) Tel. 915/MU 3-2708. Mrs. S. Harris, Libn.
Staff: 1 full time.
Size: 3,635 maps.
Annual accessions: 75 maps.
Area specialization: western Texas.
Subject specializations: geology; topography.
Depository for: USGS (topo).
Serves: public.
Interlibrary loan: not available.
Reproduction facility: Xerox.

Waco

504 BAYLOR UNIVERSITY, LIBRARY*. (76703) Tel. 817/PL 3-4511, ext. 251.
Depository for: TOPOCOM.

UTAH

Logan

505 UTAH STATE UNIVERSTIY, MERRILL LIBRARY. (84321) Tel. 801/ 752-4100, ext. 344. Max P. Peterson, Public Service Libn.
Staff: 1 part time.
Size: 3,000 maps; 41 atlases; 2 globes; 11 relief models; 13 gazetteers.
Area specialization: western United States.
Depository for: USGS (topo, geol).
Serves: University; public.
Interlibrary loan: not available.
Reproduction facility: Xerox.

Provo

506 BRIGHAM YOUNG UNIVERSITY, DOCUMENTS AND MAP LIBRARY. (84601) Harry Dees, Libn.
Staff: 1 full time; 3 part time.
Size: 32,000 maps; 650 atlases; 25 globes; 15 relief models; 363 gazetteers.
Annual accessions: 800 maps; 20 atlases; 10 gazetteers.
Area specialization: Utah.
Subject specialization: topography.
Depository for: TOPOCOM; USGS (topo).
Serves: University; public.
Interlibrary loan: available.
Reproduction facilities: photocopy; Xerox; microfilm.

Salt Lake City

507 SALT LAKE CITY PUBLIC LIBRARY, MAP SECTION, 209 East 5th South. (84111) Tel. 801/363-5733, ext. 54. Carrie Chou, Libn.
Size: 5,118 maps; 134 atlases; 2 globes; 6 relief models; 6 gazetteers.
Annual accessions: 300 maps; 15 atlases; 2 relief models.
Area specialization: Utah.
Subject specializations: geology; history.
Special cartographic collections: 190 historical maps housed in Special Collections Room (Utah Room); Utah Geological and Mineralogical Survey Publications.
Depository for: USGS (topo, geol).
Serves: public.
Interlibrary loan: available.
Reproduction facilities: photocopy; Xerox; microfilm.

508 UNIVERSITY OF UTAH LIBRARY, ENGINEERING AND PHYSICAL SCIENCE LIBRARY. (84112) Tel. 801/322-6239 or 6230. Miss Edith Rich, Engineering Libn.
Staff: 1 full time.
Size: 57,000 maps; 175 atlases; 20 relief models; 35 Braille maps.
Annual accessions: 3,000 maps; 30 atlases.
Area specializations: Utah; western United States.
Subject specializations: geology; topography.
Depository for: TOPOCOM; USGS (topo, geol).
Serves: University; public.
Interlibrary loan: not available.
Reproduction facilities: Xerox; commercial reproduction available.

Vernal

509 UTAH FIELD HOUSE OF NATURAL HISTORY, REFERENCE LIBRARY, P.O. Box 396. (84078) Tel. 801/789-3799. Billie R. Untermann, Staff Scientist.
Staff: 3 part time.
Size: 1,242 maps.
Area specializations: Utah; Rocky Mountain region.
Subject specializations: National parks and monuments; river profile maps (Green and Yampa Rivers).
Depository for: USGS (topo, geol–selective).
Serves: public.
Interlibrary loan: not available.

VERMONT

Burlington

510 UNIVERSITY OF VERMONT, GUY W. BAILEY LIBRARY, MAP
ROOM. (05401) Tel. 802/862-4993, ext. 213. David A. Cobb, Map Libn.
Staff: 1 part time.
Size: 81,250 maps; 58 atlases; 4 globes; 165 aerial photographs; 153 gazetteers.
Annual accessions: 9,000 maps; 30 atlases; 50 aerial photographs; 40 gazetteers.
Area specializations: New England; Canada.
Subject specializations: geology; topography; population.
Special cartographic collections: Civil War Maps in the Wilbur Collection;
Sanborn Insurance Maps; Canadian Urban Analysis Series.
Depository for: TOPOCOM; USGS (topo, geol); Canada; various other states.
Serves: University; public.
Interlibrary loan: not available.
Reproduction facilities: photocopy; Xerox.

Middlebury

511 MIDDLEBURY COLLEGE, MAP LIBRARY. (05753) Tel. 802/388-7002.
Dr. J. Rowland Illick, Department Chairman.
Staff: 1 part time.
Size: 60,000 maps; 50 atlases; 6 globes; 200 aerial photographs.
Annual accessions: 1,000 maps; 50 aerial photographs.
Subject specialization: topography.
Depository for: TOPOCOM; USGS (topo, geol).
Serves: College; public.
Reproduction facility: Xerox.

Northfield

512 NORWICH UNIVERSITY, HENRY PRESCOTT CHAPIN LIBRARY.
(05663) Tel. 802/485-5011, ext. 48. Mrs. Ann Turner, Public Services Libn.
Staff: 1 part time.
Size: 500 maps; 27 atlases; 2 globes; 3 gazetteers.
Special cartographic collection: U.S. Geological Survey Folios from early 20th
century (not inclusive).
Serves: University; public.
Interlibrary loan: available.
Reproduction facility: Xerox.

VIRGIN ISLANDS

Charlotte Amalie, St. Thomas.

513 ST. THOMAS PUBLIC LIBRARY. P.O. Box 390. (00801) Tel. 774-0630.
Edna M. Baa, Director of Libraries and Museums.
Size: 222 maps.
Area specialization: Caribbean Islands.
Special cartographic collection: historical maps of the Caribbean area.
Serves: public.
Interlibrary loan: not available.
Reproduction facilities: photocopy: Xerox; microfilm.

VIRGINIA

Blacksburg

514 VIRGINIA POLYTECHNIC INSTITUTE, CAROL M. NEWMAN LIBRARY. (24061) Tel. 703/552-6335. Robert E. Stephenson, Associate Libn.
Staff: 1 part time.
Size: 51,150 maps.
Annual accessions: 2,500 maps.
Area specialization: United States.
Subject specialization: geology.
Depository for: USGS (topo).
Serves: Institute; public.
Interlibrary loan: available.
Reproduction facilities: photocopy; Xerox; microfilm.
Publication: Guide to the Map Collection in the Carol M. Newman Library by Frank C. Shirk. 1961.

Bridgewater

515 BRIDGEWATER COLLEGE, ALEXANDER MACK MEMORIAL LIBRARY. (22812) Tel. 703/828-2011, ext. 91. Orland Wages, Libn.
Staff: 1 part time.
Size: 1,117 maps; 36 atlases; 2 globes; 2 relief models; 4 gazetteers.
Depository for: USGS (topo).
Serves: College; public.
Reproduction facility: photocopy.

Charlottesville

516 UNIVERSITY OF VIRGINIA, ALDERMAN LIBRARY*. (22901) Tel. 703/295-2166.
Size: 122,890 maps.
Depository for: TOPOCOM.

Hampden-Sydney

517 HAMPDEN-SYDNEY COLLEGE, EGGLESTON LIBRARY. (23943) Tel. 703/223-4371. Mrs. Florence P. Seamster.
Staff: 1 part time.
Size: 708 maps; 20 atlases; 4 gazetteers.
Annual accessions: 50 maps; 3 atlases.
Area specialization: Virginia.
Subject specialization: Civil War.
Depository for: USGS (topo—Virginia).
Serves: College; public.
Interlibrary loan: not available.

Newport News

518 MARINERS' MUSEUM, LIBRARY. (23606) Tel. 703/595-0368. John Lochhead, Libn.
Size: 1,625 maps; 230 atlases; 8 globes.
Serves: public.
Interlibrary loan: not available.
Reproduction facility: photocopy.

Portsmouth

519 PORTSMOUTH NAVAL SHIPYARD MUSEUM, INC., 2 High Street
(P.O. Box 248). (23703) Tel. 703/393-6009. Marshall W. Butt, Director.
Staff: 2 full time.
Size: 150 maps; 1 relief model; 2 gazetteers.
Area specializations: Portsmouth and vicinity.
Special cartographic collection: collection of Portsmouth area maps, mostly
photocopies, dating from 1752.
Serves: Museum.
Interlibrary loan: not available.

Richmond

520 CONFEDERATE MUSEUM LIBRARY, 1201 East Clay Street. (23219)
Tel. 703/648-8133. Eleanor S. Brockenbrough, Assistant Director.
Staff: 1 part time.
Size: 225 maps.
Area specialization: Confederate States.
Subject specializations: history; Civil War.
Serves: public (by permission).
Interlibrary loan: not available.

521 VALENTINE MUSEUM, RESEARCH LIBRARY, 1015 East Clay Street.
(23219) Tel. 703/649-0711. Mrs. Stuart Gibson, Libn.
Staff: 2 full time.
Size: 100 maps; 8 atlases; 2 globes.
Area specializations: Richmond; Virginia.
Subject specialization: history.
Serves: public.
Interlibrary loan: available (restricted).

522 VIRGINIA HISTORICAL SOCIETY, P.O. Box 7311. (23221) Tel. 703/358-
4901. Howson W. Cole, Curator of Manuscripts.
Staff: 2 part time.
Size: 2,000 maps; 100 atlases; 10 gazetteers.
Annual accessions: 100 maps.
Area specialization: Virginia.
Special cartographic collection: Jeremy Francis Gilmer Civil War Maps of
Virginia.
Serves: public.
Interlibrary loan: not available.
Reproduction facilities: photocopy; Xerox.

523 VIRGINIA STATE LIBRARY. (23219) Tel. 703/770-2308.
Staff: 1 part time.
Size: 56,000 maps; 150 atlases.
Annual accessions: 2,000 maps; 2 atlases.
Area specialization: Virginia.
Special cartographic collection: Board of Public Works manuscript maps relating to
19th century Virginia internal improvements (roads, canals, railroads, etc.).
Depository for: TOPOCOM; USGS (topo).
Serves: public.
Interlibrary loan: not available.
Reproduction facilities: photocopy; Xerox; microfilm.

WASHINGTON

Bellingham

524 WESTERN WASHINGTON STATE COLLEGE, DEPARTMENT OF GEOGRAPHY, MAP LIBRARY. (98225) Tel. 206/734-8800, ext. 1493. Miss Kathleen Brennan, Map Curator.

Staff: 1 full time; 3 part time.

Size: 47,000 maps; 37 atlases; 38 globes; 60 relief models; 4,075 aerial photographs; 77 gazetteers.

Annual accessions: 2,700 maps; 6 gazetteers.

Area specializations: Pacific Northwest; Alaska; western Canada.

Subject specializations: urban planning; economic geography.

Depository for: TOPOCOM; USGS (topo).

Serves: College; public.

Interlibrary loan: available.

Reproduction facility: Xerox.

Cheney

525 EASTERN WASHINGTON STATE COLLEGE, GEOGRAPHY DEPARTMENT. (99004). Tel. 509/359-2547. Mr. Dale Stradling.

Staff: 2 part time.

Size: 15,000 maps; 20 atlases; 10 globes; 100 relief models; 50 aerial photographs; 10 gazetteers.

Annual accessions: 1,000 maps.

Subject specializations: city planning; topography.

Serves: College.

Interlibrary loan: available.

Reproduction facilities: photocopy; Xerox.

Ellensburg

526 CENTRAL WASHINGTON STATE COLLEGE, LIBRARY, DOCUMENTS SECTION, MAP ROOM. (98926) Tel. 509/963-1541. Mrs. Ruth Dahlgren Hartman, Documents Libn.

Staff: 3 part time.

Size: 10,666 maps; 50 atlases; 5 globes; 110 gazetteers.

Annual accessions: 2,188 maps; 10 atlases; 10 gazetteers.

Area specialization: United States.

Subject specializations: geology; topography.

Depository for: TOPOCOM (partial); USGS (topo, geol).

Serves: College; public.

Interlibrary loan: available (restricted).

Reproduction facilities: photocopy; Xerox.

Pullman

527 WASHINGTON STATE UNIVERSITY, DEPARTMENT OF GEOLOGY. (99163). Tel. 509/ED 5-3009.

Staff: 1 part time.

Size: not reported.

Area specialization: United States.

Subject specializations: geology; topography.

Depository for: USGS (topo, geol).

Serves: University.
Interlibrary loan: available.

528   WASHINGTON STATE UNIVERSITY, LIBRARY. (99163) Tel. 509/ED 5-4539. Mrs. Margaret Hilty, Social Science Library; Betty Roberts, Science Library; Earle Connette, Archives.

Size: 1,976 maps (Science Library); 500 maps (Archives); 34 atlases; 9 relief models; 1,500 aerial photographs (Science Library); 4 gazetteers.

Special cartographic collections: 500 maps relating to the discovery and development of the Pacific Northwest; Father de Smet's original maps; Soil Conservation Service maps; World Aeronautical Charts.

Depository for: TOPOCOM; USGS (topo—western states only).

Serves: University; public.

Interlibrary loan: not available.

Reproduction facilities: photocopy; Xerox.

Seattle

529   SEATTLE PUBLIC LIBRARY, HISTORY DEPARTMENT, 4th and Madison. (98104) Tel. 206/MA 4-3800, ext. 220. Diane Westman.

Staff: 1 part time.

Size: 1,639 maps (plus those received on deposit); 155 atlases; 1 globe; 25 gazetteers.

Annual accessions: 100 maps; 6 globes.

Area specialization: Pacific Northwest.

Depository for: TOPOCOM; USGS (topo).

Serves: public.

Interlibrary loan: not available.

Reproduction facilities: photocopy; Xerox.

530   UNIVERSITY OF WASHINGTON, FISHERIES-OCEANOGRAPHY LIBRARY, 151 Oceanography Teaching Building. (98105) Tel. 206/543-4279. Raymond E. Durrance, Libn.

Size: 1,000 maps; 30 atlases; 50 aerial photographs; 10 gazetteers.

Annual accessions: 60 maps; 5 atlases; 5 aerial photographs.

Area specialization: North American coastal areas.

Subject specializations: oceanography; bathymetry.

Depository for: USGS (topo).

Serves: University; public.

Interlibrary loan: available.

Reproduction facilities: photocopy; Xerox; microfilm.

531   UNIVERSITY OF WASHINGTON, GEOGRAPHY AND MAP LIBRARY. (98105) Tel. 206/543-5244. Elinor C. Kelly, Libn.

Staff: 1 full time; 4 part time.

Size: 182,000 maps; 456 atlases; 4 globes; 95 relief models; 175 gazetteers.

Annual accessions: 7,000 maps; 50 atlases; 5 relief models; 6 gazetteers.

Area specializations: Washington; western United States; USSR.

Subject specialization: comprehensive.

Depository for: TOPOCOM.

Serves: University; public.

Interlibrary loan: available.

Reproduction facilities: photocopy; Xerox; microfilm.

532 UNIVERSITY OF WASHINGTON, LIBRARY, SCIENCE READING ROOM. (98105) Tel. 206/543-1243. Helen Strickland, Science Libn.
Staff: 1 part time.
Size: 25,000 maps.
Annual accessions: 1,700 maps.
Subject specialization: geology.
Depository for: USGS (topo, geol).
Serves: University; public.
Reproduction facilities: photocopy; Xerox; microfilm.

Spokane

533 EASTERN WASHINGTON STATE HISTORICAL SOCIETY, 2316 W. First Avenue. (99204) Tel. 509/MA 4-3225. Mabel Turner, Libn.
Size: 200 maps; 10 atlases; 1 globe.
Annual accessions: 10 maps.
Area specialization: Pacific Northwest.
Subject specialization: local history.
Serves: public.
Interlibrary loan: available.
Reproduction facility: photocopy.

534 SPOKANE PUBLIC LIBRARY, REFERENCE DEPARTMENT, W 906 Main Avenue. (99201) Tel. 509/MA 4-4201. Mrs. Martha Anderson, Libn.
Staff: 2 part time.
Size: 6,000 maps; 50 atlases; 3 globes; 3 relief models; 107 gazetteers.
Annual accessions: 600 maps; 5 atlases.
Area specialization: Pacific Northwest.
Subject specialization: local history.
Depository for: USGS (topo,geol—Pacific Northwest states).
Serves: public.
Interlibrary loan: available.
Reproduction facility: photocopy.

Tacoma

535 PACIFIC LUTHERAN UNIVERSITY, Parkland. (98447) Tel. 206/LE 1-6900, ext. 301. Brian Lowes.
Staff: 1 part time.
Size: 600 maps; 2 atlases; 2 globes; 24 relief models; 100 aerial photographs.
Annual accessions: 100 maps.
Subject specializations: geomorphology; geology; cultural geography.
Depository for: USGS (topo).
Serves: University; public.
Reproduction facilities: photocopy; Xerox; Ozalid.

536 UNIVERSITY OF PUGET SOUND, GEOLOGY DEPARTMENT, 1500 North Warner. (98416) Tel. 206/SK 9-3521, ext. 729. Norman R. Anderson, Department Head.
Staff: 2 part time.
Size: 15,000 maps; 75 relief models; 200 aerial photographs.
Annual accessions: 1,000 maps.
Area specialization: western United States.
Subject specialization: geology.

Depository for: USGS (topo).
Serves: University; public.
Interlibrary loan: not available.

537 WASHINGTON STATE HISTORICAL SOCIETY LIBRARY, 315 North Stadium Way. (98403) Tel. 206/FU 3-2509. Frank L. Green, Libn.
Size: 500 maps.
Area specializations: Tacoma; Pierce County; Pacific Northwest.
Subject specializations: discovery and exploration; trails.
Special cartographic collection: Buckmaster Collection of historical maps.
Serves: public.
Interlibrary loan: not available.

Walla Walla

538 WHITMAN COLLEGE, PENROSE MEMORIAL LIBRARY. (99362) Tel. 509/JA 9-5100. ext. 265 or 266. Mrs. Martha Jacky, Assistant Libn.
Size: 2,547 maps.
Depository for: TOPOCOM; USGS (topo, geol).
Serves: College; public.
Interlibrary loan: not available.
Reproduction facilities: photocopy; Xerox.

WEST VIRGINIA

Charleston

539 WEST VIRGINIA (STATE) DEPARTMENT OF ARCHIVES AND HISTORY, Room E-400, Capitol Building. (25305) Tel. 304/348-2277.
Size: 3,000 maps; 175 atlases; 100 gazetteers.
Area specializations: West Virginia; Virginia.
Subject specializations: history; geology.
Depository for: USGS (topo, geol).
Serves: public.
Interlibrary loan: not available.

Morgantown

540 WEST VIRGINIA (STATE) GEOLOGICAL AND ECONOMIC SURVEY, LIBRARY. (26505) Tel. 304/296-4461. Ruth I. Hayhurst, Libn.
Staff: 1 part time.
Size: 10,000 maps.
Annual accessions: 450 maps.
Area specialization: West Virginia.
Subject specializations: geology; natural resources.
Depository for: USGS (topo,geol—West Virginia).
Serves: employees; public.
Interlibrary loan: not available.
Reproduction facility: photocopy.

541 WEST VIRGINIA UNIVERSITY, LIBRARY*. (26506)
Depository for: TOPOCOM.

542 WEST VIRGINIA UNIVERSITY, LIBRARY, WEST VIRGINIA COLLECTION. (26506) Tel. 304/293-2240. A.D. Mastrogiuseppe, Assistant Curator.
Size: 1,500 maps; 18,000 aerial photographs.

Area specializations: West Virginia; Ohio; Virginia.
Serves: University; public.
Interlibrary loan: not available.
Reproduction facilities: photocopy; Xerox; microfilm.

WISCONSIN

Appleton

543   LAWRENCE UNIVERSITY, LIBRARY*. (54911) Tel. 414/739-3681.
Depository for: TOPOCOM.

Beloit

544   BELOIT COLLEGE, LIBRARY. (53511) Tel. 608/365-3391, ext. 230. C.
Peterman, Associate Director.
Staff: 1 part time.
Size: 54,166 maps; 32 atlases; 1 globe; 11 gazetteers.
Annual accessions: 3,000 maps; 5 atlases.
Subject specializations: topography; geology.
Depository for: TOPOCOM; USGS (topo, geol).
Serves: College; public.
Interlibrary loan: available.
Reproduction facility: Xerox.

Kenosha

545   KENOSHA COUNTY HISTORICAL SOCIETY, 6300 Third Avenue.
(53140) Tel. 414/654-5770. Sue Vedder, Libn.
Staff: 1 part time.
Size: 150 maps; 20 atlases.
Annual accessions: 50 maps; 5 atlases.
Area specializations: Wisconsin; Kenosha, Racine, and Milwaukee counties.
Subject specialization: local history.
Serves: public.
Interlibrary loan: not available.
Reproduction facility: Xerox.

La Crosse

546   WISCONSIN STATE UNIVERSITY AT LA CROSSE, GEOGRAPHY
DEPARTMENT, MAP LIBRARY. (54601) Tel. 608/785-1800, ext. 250.
Jerry B. Culver.
Staff: 1 part time.
Size: 5,000 maps; 80 globes; 12 relief models.
Annual accessions: 150 maps.
Area specializations: Wisconsin; midwestern United States.
Subject specializations: geography; topography.
Serves: University; public.
Interlibrary loan: not available.
Reproduction facility: photocopy.

Madison

547 STATE HISTORICAL SOCIETY OF WISCONSIN, DIVISION OF ARCHIVES AND MANUSCRIPTS, MAP LIBRARY. (53706) Tel. 608/ 262-3338. Mrs. Margaret Hafstad, Manuscripts Curator.

Staff: 1 part time.
Size: 45,200 maps; 2,050 atlases.
Annual accessions: 1,325 maps; 30 atlases.
Area specializations: Wisconsin; United States.
Subject specializations: history; genealogy.
Special cartographic collection: Sanborn insurance maps of Wisconsin cities.
Depository for: USGS (topo).
Serves: public.
Interlibrary loan: not available.
Reproduction facilities: photocopy; Xerox; microfilm.

548 UNIVERSITY OF WISCONSIN, MAP AND AIR PHOTO LIBRARY, 384 Science Hall. (53706) Tel. 608/262-1804. Miss Mary Galneder, Map Libn.

Staff: 1 full time; 2 part time.
Size: 113,250 maps; 10 atlases; 1 globe; 280 relief models; 67,000 aerial photographs; 240 gazetteers.
Annual accessions: 5,700 maps; 2,000 aerial photographs; 15 gazetteers.
Area specialization: comprehensive.
Subject specialization: comprehensive.
Depository for: TOPOCOM; USGS (topo, geol).
Serves: University; public.
Interlibrary loan: not available.
Reproduction facility: Xerox.
Note: Atlases and other reference materials are found in the Geology-Geography Library located in the same building.

Milwaukee

549 MILWAUKEE PUBLIC LIBRARY, 814 West Wisconsin Avenue. (53233) Tel. 414/276-7578, ext. 247. Peter J. McCormick.

Size: 65,000 maps; 350 atlases; 2 globes; 250 gazetteers.
Annual accessions: 2,500 maps.
Area specializations: Milwaukee; Wisconsin.
Subject specializations: local history; soils; geology; topography.
Depository for: TOPOCOM; USGS (topo, geol).
Serves: public.
Interlibrary loan: not available.
Reproduction facilities: photocopy; Xerox.

550 UNIVERSITY OF WISCONSIN AT MILWAUKEE, GEOGRAPHY DEPARTMENT, MAP LIBRARY, Room 379, Sabin Hall. (53201) Tel. 414/228-4866. Mrs. Olive Murray, Map Libn.

Staff: 3 full time.
Size: 86,923 maps; 616 wall maps; 8 atlases; 1 globe; 50 relief models; 300 aerial photographs; 30 gazetteers.
Annual accessions: 5,000 maps; 25 wall maps.
Subject specializations: urban and planning cartography.
Depository for: TOPOCOM; USGS (topo, geol); USC&GS.
Serves: University; public.

Interlibrary loan: not available.
Reproduction facilities: Xerox; Ozalid.

Platteville

551 WISCONSIN STATE UNIVERSITY AT PLATTEVILLE, ELTON S. KARRMANN LIBRARY. (53818) Tel. 608/348-2037. David J. Lamb, Engineering and Technology Division Libn.
Staff: 1 part time.
Size: 2,224 maps; 45 atlases; 2 globes; 1 relief model; 2 gazetteers.
Annual accessions: 434 maps; 4 atlases.
Area specialization: southwestern Wisconsin.
Subject specialization: geology.
Depository for: TOPOCOM.
Serves: University; public.
Interlibrary loan: available.
Reproduction facilities: Xerox; microfilm.

Racine

552 RACINE PUBLIC LIBRARY, 75 7th Street. (53403)
Size: maps not reported; 120 atlases; 1 globe; 19 gazetteers.
Depository for: USGS (topo, geol—Wisconsin).
Serves: public.
Interlibrary loan: available.
Reproduction facility: Thermofax.

Stevens Point

553 WISCONSIN STATE UNIVERSITY AT STEVENS POINT, DEPARTMENT OF GEOGRAPHY. (54481) Tel. 715/351-1251, ext. 353. Maurice Perret, Curator.
Staff: 3 part time.
Size: 60,000 maps; 10 atlases; 10 globes; 250 relief models; 200 aerial photographs; 25 gazetteers.
Annual accessions: 500 maps; 30 relief models; 50 aerial photographs.
Depository for: TOPOCOM; USGS (topo).
Serves: University; public.
Interlibrary loan: available.
Reproduction facility: Xerox.

Superior

554 WISCONSIN STATE UNIVERSITY AT SUPERIOR, JIM DAN HILL LIBRARY. (54880) Tel. 715/392-8101. Edward F. Greve, Reference Libn.
Size: 1,200 maps; 57 atlases; 1 globe; 30 gazetteers.
Area specialization: Wisconsin.
Subject specializations: geology; topography.
Serves: University; public.
Interlibrary loan: not available.
Reproduction facility: Xerox.

Waukesha

555 SOUTHEASTERN WISCONSIN REGIONAL PLANNING COMMISSION, CARTOGRAPHIC AND DESIGN DIVISION, 916 North East Avenue. (53186) Tel. 414/542-8083. Dallas R. Behnke, Mapping Division.
Size: 800 maps; 1,450 aerial photographs.
Area specialization: southeastern Wisconsin cities and towns.
Subject specializations: land use; transportation; urban and regional planning.
Special cartographic collection: large scale county base maps.
Serves: public.
Interlibrary loan: available.
Reproduction facilities: Xerox; Diazo.

Whitewater

556 WISCONSIN STATE UNIVERSITY AT WHITEWATER, DEPARTMENT OF GEOGRAPHY*, Upham Hall. (53190).
Depository for: TOPOCOM.

WYOMING

Cheyenne

557 WYOMING STATE ENGINEERS OFFICE, State Office Building. (82001) Tel. 307/777-7354. Lola B. Lindsay, Libn.
Staff: 1 full time.
Size: 37,000 maps.
Annual accessions: 400 maps.
Area specialization: Wyoming.
Subject specialization: water rights.
Depository for: USGS (topo).
Serves: public.
Reproduction facilities: Xerox; microfilm.

558 WYOMING STATE LIBRARY, Supreme Court Building. (82001) Tel. 307/777-7281, ext. 29. Alice Lane, Head, Documents Department.
Size: 2,500 maps; 15 atlases; 2 globes; 2 relief models; 5 gazetteers.
Area specializations: Wyoming; western United States.
Subject specializations: geology; recreation; mineral resources; history.
Depository for: USGS (topo); State of Wyoming.
Serves: public.
Interlibrary loan: available.
Reproduction facility: Xerox.

559 WYOMING (STATE) NATURAL RESOURCE BOARD, 210 West 23rd Street. (82001) Tel. 307/777-7284.
Size: 1,500 maps; 25 relief models; 2,000 aerial photographs.
Annual accessions: 100 maps.
Area specializations: Wyoming; western United States.
Subject specializations: geology; topography; water resources; mineral resources.
Depository for: USGS (topo); Wyoming county highway maps.
Serves: public.
Interlibrary loan: not available.
Reproduction facility: Xerox.

Laramie

560 UNIVERSITY OF WYOMING, GEOLOGY LIBRARY. (82070) Tel. 307/ 766-3374. Mrs. Teresa Robinson, Libn.
Staff: 1 full time; 2 part time.
Size: 4,000 maps; 20 atlases; 1 relief model; 20 sets of aerial photographs.
Annual accessions: 300 maps; 2 atlases.
Subject specializations: geology; topography.
Depository for: USGS (topo, geol—Wyoming).
Serves: University.
Interlibrary loan: available.
Reproduction facility: Xerox.

561 UNIVERSITY OF WYOMING, LIBRARY, DOCUMENTS DIVISION. (82070) Tel. 307/766-2174. Irene Gedda, Documents Libn.
Staff: 1 part time.
Size: 45,000 maps; 400 atlases; 19 relief models; 100 aerial photographs; 41 weather maps on film.
Annual accessions: 2,600 maps; 10 atlases; 2 relief models.
Area specializations: Wyoming; western United States.
Subject specializations: geology; topography; history.
Depository for: TOPOCOM; USGS (topo, geol).
Serves: University; public.
Interlibrary loan: available.

Sheridan

562 SHERIDAN COLLEGE, KOOI LIBRARY. (82801) Tel. 307/674-4421, ext. 6. Holly V. Ohm, Libn.
Staff: 1 part time.
Size: 1,640 maps.
Depository for: USGS (topo, geol).
Serves: College; public.
Interlibrary loan: not available.
Reproduction facility: photocopy.

ALBERTA

Calgary

563 CALGARY PUBLIC LIBRARY, BUSINESS, SCIENCE AND TECH-
NOLOGY, 616 MacLeod Trail S.E., (21). Tel. 403/263-1820.
Size: 15,000 maps; 200 atlases; 1 globe; 10 books of aerial photographs (Alberta);
30 gazetteers.
Annual accessions: 400 maps; 20 atlases; 20 gazetteers.
Area specializations: Canada; Alberta; Alaska; Australia.
Subject specializations: geosciences; petroleum; topography; mineral resources.
Serves: public.
Interlibrary loan: not available.
Reproduction facility: Xerox.

564 UNIVERSITY OF CALGARY, LIBRARY, MAP LIBRARY, (44) Tel.
403/284-5969. Miss Caroline Grummitt, Map Specialist.
Staff: 1 full time.
Size: 22,000 maps; 450 atlases; 1 globe; 40 gazetteers.
Area specializations: Canada; Latin America.
Depository for: USGS (topo, geol); Canada (NTS); DOS.
Serves: University; public.
Reproduction facilities: photocopy; Xerox.
Publication: quarterly accessions list.

Edmonton

565 UNIVERSITY OF ALBERTA, DEPARTMENT OF GEOGRAPHY,
UNIVERSITY MAP COLLECTION. H. L. P. Stibbe, Map Curator.
Staff: 2 full time.
Size: 50,000 maps; 300 atlases; 7 globes; 55 relief models; 130,000 aerial
photographs.
Area specialization: northern lands.
Depository for: Canada; DOS; Alberta Province; Ontario Province.
Serves: University; public.
Interlibrary loan: not available.
Reproduction facilities: photocopy; Xerox.

BRITISH COLUMBIA

Burnaby

566 SIMON FRASER UNIVERSITY, LIBRARY, SOCIAL SCIENCE DIVI-
SION, (2). Tel. 604/291-3283. Brian Phillips, Division Head.
Staff: 1 full time; 1 part time.
Size: 20,000 maps; 600 atlases; 1,000 aerial photographs; 40 gazetteers.
Annual accessions: 3,000 maps.
Area specializations: Canada; North America; central Africa.
Depository for: Canada.
Serves: University; public.
Interlibrary loan: available.
Reproduction facility: Xerox.

Vancouver

567 UNIVERSITY OF BRITISH COLUMBIA, DEPARTMENT OF GEOG-
RAPHY, MAP LIBRARY, (8) Tel. 604/228-3048. Josef Schonfeld, Map
Libn.
Staff: 1 full time.
Size: 51,000 maps; 16,600 aerial photographs; 70 gazetteers.
Annual accessions: 4,000 maps; 140 aerial photographs.
Depository for: Canada.
Serves: University; public.
Reproduction facility: photocopy.

568 UNIVERSITY OF BRITISH COLUMBIA, LIBRARY, MAP DIVISION,
(8) Tel. 604/228-2231. Miss Maureen F. Wilson, Head, Map Division.
Staff: 3 full time; 4 part time.
Size: 61,000 maps; 1,004 atlases; 3 globes; 1 relief model; 185 gazetteers.
Annual accessions: 5,000 maps.
Area specializations: British Columbia; Canada; Africa; Alaska.
Depository for: Canadian Hydrographic Service; USC&GS; DOS; British Columbia
Department of Lands, Forests, and Water Resources.
Serves: University; public.
Interlibrary loan: available.
Reproduction facilities: photocopy; Xerox.
Publications: brochure, accessions list (bimonthly).

569 UNIVERSITY OF BRITISH COLUMBIA, LIBRARY, SPECIAL COL-
LECTIONS DIVISION, (8) Tel. 604/228-2521. Miss Frances Woodward,
Reference Libn.
Staff: 2 part time.
Size: 1,500 maps; 159 atlases; 40 gazetteers.
Area specializations: British Columbia; Canada; North America.
Subject specialization: historical cartography.
Serves: University; public.
Interlibrary loan: not available.
Reproduction facilities: photocopy; Xerox; microfilm.
Publication: accessions list at irregular intervals.

Victoria

570 GREATER VICTORIA PUBLIC LIBRARY, REFERENCE DEPART-
MENT, 1312 Blanshard Street. Tel. 604/382-7241. Terence Curran, Assist-
ant Department Head.
Size: 450 maps; 40 atlases; 2 globes; 1 relief model; 15 gazetteers.
Annual accessions: 30 maps; 2 atlases.
Area specialization: British Columbia.
Depository for: British Columbia.
Serves: public.
Interlibrary loan: not available.
Reproduction facility: photocopy.

571 PROVINCIAL ARCHIVES OF BRITISH COLUMBIA, MAP DIVISION,
Parliament Buildings. Tel. 604/382-6111, local 2505. Miss Frances Gundry,
Libn.
Size: 9,000 maps; 120 atlases; 3 globes; 24 gazetteers.
Annual accessions: 200 maps.
Area specializations: British Columbia; Pacific Northwest.
Subject specialization: history.

Depository for: Canadian Hydrographic Service; British Columbia.
Serves: public.
Interlibrary loan: not available.
Reproduction facilities: photocopy; Xerox; microfilm.

572   UNIVERSITY OF VICTORIA, GEOGRAPHY DEPARTMENT, LI-
BRARY, Room 142, Cornett Building, P.O. Box 1700. Tel. 604/477-6911,
local 228. Mrs. Barbara Mordaunt, Geography Library Assistant.
Staff: 1 full time; 3 part time.
Size: 28,000 maps; 30 atlases; 12,000 aerial photographs; 2 gazetteers.
Annual accessions: 1200 maps; 5 atlases.
Area specializations: Canada; Australia; New Zealand.
Subject specialization: topography.
Depository for: Canada; Australia; DOS.
Serves: University; public.
Interlibrary loan: not available.
Reproduction facility: Xerox.

MANITOBA

Winnipeg

573   PROVINCIAL LIBRARY AND ARCHIVES OF MANITOBA, Room 247,
Legislative Building, (1) Tel. 204/946-1765, Miss Elizabeth Blight.
Staff: 1 part time.
Size: 800 maps; 30 atlases;1 globe; 1 relief model; 500 aerial photographs; 50
gazetteers.
Area specialization: Manitoba.
Special cartographic collection: historical maps of Manitoba and the Canadian
West.
Serves: public.
Interlibrary loan: not available.
Reproduction facility: microfilm.

574   UNIVERSITY OF MANITOBA, ELIZABETH DAFOE LIBRARY, (19)
Tel. 204/474-9844, Miss Sharon Tully, Map and Reference Libn.
Staff: 1 part time.
Size: 20,000 maps; 300 atlases; 1 globe; 10 relief models; 35 gazetteers.
Annual accessions: 3,000 maps; 100 atlases; 5 gazetteers.
Area specializations: Canada; United States; Europe.
Subject specialization: topography.
Depository for: USGS (topo); Canada (NTS).
Serves: University; public.
Interlibrary loan: available.
Reproduction facility: Xerox.
Publication: monthly acquisitions list (maps).

NEW BRUNSWICK

Fredericton

575   UNIVERSITY OF NEW BRUNSWICK, HARRIET IRVING LIBRARY.
Tel. 506/475-9471, ext. 381. Mrs. Judith Colson, Government Documents
Libn.

Size: 2,000 maps; some atlases; some gazetteers.
Area specializations: New Brunswick; Canada.
Special cartographic collection: pre-1900 maps of New Brunswick and the Maritime Provinces.
Depository for: Canada.
Serves: University; public.
Interlibrary loan: available.

NOVA SCOTIA

Halifax

576 DALHOUSIE UNIVERSITY, SCIENCE LIBRARY, Sir James Dunn Science Building. Tel. 902/424-3581. Mrs. Linda Harvey, Assistant Libn.
Staff: 1 part time.
Size: 10,000 maps; 30 atlases; 10 gazetteers.
Annual accessions: 500 maps; 5 atlases; 2 gazetteers.
Area specialization: Maritime Provinces of Canada.
Subject specialization: geology.
Depository for: USGS (topo, geol); USC&GS; Canada.
Serves: University; public.
Interlibrary loan: available.
Reproduction facility: photocopy.

ONTARIO

Haileybury

577 NORTHERN COLLEGE OF APPLIED ARTS AND TECHNOLOGY, SCHOOL OF MINES, Haileybury Campus, P.O. Box 428. Tel. 705/672-3414. Mrs. C. E. Neelands, Libn.
Staff: 1 part time.
Size: not reported.
Subject specializations: geology; geophysics.
Depository for: Canada (GSC); Ontario Department of Mines.
Serves: College; public.
Interlibrary loan: not available.

Hamilton

578 McMASTER UNIVERSITY, MILLS MEMORIAL LIBRARY, MAP LIBRARY, Room 311. Tel. 416/522-4971, local 537. Mrs. Kate Donkin, Map Curator.
Staff: 2 full time.
Size: 50,000 maps; 100 atlases; 1 globe; 2 gazetteers.
Annual accessions: 3,000 maps; 25 atlases.
Area specializations: southern Ontario; Niagara Peninsula.
Subject specializations: history; geography.
Depository for: Canada.
Serves: University.
Interlibrary loan: available (restricted).
Reproduction facilities: photocopy; microfilm.

Kingston

579 QUEEN'S UNIVERSITY, DEPARTMENT OF GEOGRAPHY, MAP AND AIR PHOTO LIBRARY. Tel. 613/546-3871, ext. 439. Mrs. Helen L. Allen, Map Curator.
Staff: 1 full time; 1 part time.
Size: 36,000 maps; 225 atlases; 12,500 aerial photographs; 75 gazetteers.
Annual accessions: 3,000 maps; 25 atlases; 1,500 aerial photographs; 10 gazetteers.
Area specializations: eastern Ontario; Canada; Africa.
Subject specializations: economic and human geography; soils.
Depository for: USGS (topo—selective); Canada; DOS.
Serves: University; public.

580 QUEEN'S UNIVERSITY, DOUGLAS LIBRARY, SPECIAL COLLECTIONS, MAP COLLECTION. Tel. 613/546-3871, ext. 191. William F. E. Morley, Special Collections Curator.
Staff: 1 part time.
Size: 450 maps; 90 atlases; 1 globe; 50 gazetteers.
Area specializations: Canada; North America.
Subject specialization: historical cartography.
Special cartographic collections: 19th century atlases of Ontario; 17th and 18th century maps illustrating the discovery and exploration of Canada.
Serves: University; public.
Interlibrary loan: available.
Reproduction facilities: photocopy; Xerox; microfilm.

London

581 UNIVERSITY OF WESTERN ONTARIO, DEPARTMENT OF GEOGRAPHY, MAP COLLECTION. Tel. 519/679-3424. S. A. Sauer, Map Curator.
Staff: 1 full time; 2 part time.
Size: 53,000 maps; 320 atlases; 6 globes; 416 relief models; 8,000 aerial photographs; 54 gazetteers.
Annual accessions: 21,000 maps; 60 atlases; 3 globes; 1,500 aerial photographs; 22 gazetteers.
Area specializations: Canada; United States; Latin America.
Depository for: USGS (topo): USC&GS; Canada (NTS); Canadian Hydrographic Service; Canada Land Inventory.
Serves: University; public.
Interlibrary loan: not available.
Reproduction facilities: Xerox; microprinter.

Ottawa

582 DEPARTMENT OF ENERGY, MINES AND RESOURCES, DEPARTMENTAL MAP LIBRARY, (4) Tel. 613/994-4911. Lorne B. Leafloor, Head, Departmental Map Library.
Staff: 3 full time; 1 part time.
Size: 100,000 maps; 1,000 atlases; 15 globes; 2 relief models; 850 gazetteers.
Annual accessions: 3,000 maps; 25 atlases; 5 globes; 10 gazetteers.
Area specialization: comprehensive.
Subject specialization: topography.
Depository for: Canada.
Serves: public.
Interlibrary loan: available (some restrictions).

Reproduction facilities: photocopy; Xerox.
Publications: Accession List; Map Source List.

583 GEOLOGICAL SURVEY OF CANADA, LIBRARY, Room 350, 601
Booth Street. Tel. 613/994-5257. Mrs. D. M. Sutherland, Chief Libn.
Staff: 1 part time.
Size: 40,000 maps; 50 atlases; 2 globes; 2 gazetteers.
Annual accessions: 2,000 maps.
Area specialization: comprehensive.
Subject specialization: geology.
Serves: public.
Interlibrary loan: available.

584 PUBLIC ARCHIVES OF CANADA, MAP DIVISION, NATIONAL MAP
COLLECTION, 395 Wellington Street, (4) Tel. 613/992-0468. T. E. Layng,
Chief, Map Division.
Staff: 13 full time.
Size: 461,017 maps; 1,847 atlases; 5 globes; 150 gazetteers.
Annual accessions: 65,000 maps; 25 atlases; 10 gazetteers.
Area specialization: Canada.
Special cartographic collections: Des Barres' *The Atlantic Neptune*; Murray Map
1760 (French Canada).
Depository for: Canada (NTS).
Serves: public.
Interlibrary loan: available (restricted).
Reproduction facilities: photocopy; Xerox; microfilm.

585 SOIL RESEARCH INSTITUTE, CARTOGRAPHIC MAP REFERENCE
LIBRARY, CARTOGRAPHIC SECTION, Central Experimental Farm.
Tel. 613/994-9447 or 5247. Nelson J. Towers, Cartography Libn.
Staff: 1 full time; 1 part time.
Size: 24,000 maps; 7 atlases.
Area specializations: Canada; North America.
Subject specializations: soils; topography; economic geography; climatology.
Serves: Institute; public.
Interlibrary loan: available.
Reproduction facilities: Xerox; Diazo.

586 UNIVERSITY OF OTTAWA, DEPARTMENT OF GEOGRAPHY, MAP
LIBRARY. Tel. 613/231-3948. Miss Beverly L. Drouillard, Map Libn.
Staff: 1 full time; 2 part time.
Size: 20,269 flat maps; 68 wall maps; 117 atlases; 1 globe; 16 relief models; 13,324
aerial photographs; 8 gazetteers.
Area specialization: Canada.
Special cartographic collection: complete aerial photographic coverage for Ottawa
and Montreal and partial coverage for the St. Lawrence Seaway, eastern
Quebec Province, and Nova Scotia.
Depository for: Canada (NTS).
Serves: University.
Interlibrary loan: available (restricted).

Sudbury

587 LAURENTIAN UNIVERSITY, LIBRARY, MAP LIBRARY. Tel. 705/
675-1151, ext. 334. Mrs. José Wright.
Staff: 1 part time.

Size: 1,100 maps; 45 atlases; 10 gazetteers.
Area specializations: Ontario; Canada.
Subject specialization: geology.
Depository for: Canada.
Serves: University; public.
Interlibrary loan: available.
Reproduction facility: Xerox.

Toronto

588 METROPOLITAN TORONTO CENTRAL LIBRARY, St. George and College Streets, (2B) Tel. 416/924-9511. Michael Pearson, Head, History Section.
Staff: 3 part time.
Size: 10,000 maps; 250 atlases; 200 gazetteers.
Annual accessions: 75 maps; 15 atlases; 10 gazetteers.
Area specializations: Toronto; Ontario; Canada.
Subject specializations: topography; geology.
Depository for: Canada.
Serves: public.
Interlibrary loan: available (restricted).
Reproduction facilities: Xerox; photocopying and microfilming available commercially.

589 ONTARIO DEPARTMENT OF LANDS AND FORESTS, LANDS AND SURVEYS BRANCH–SURVEYS SECTION, MAP DISTRIBUTION AND SURVEY RECORDS, Whitney Block, Parliament Buildings, (5) Tel. 416/365-2724. W. E. Carroll, Executive Officer.
Size: 1,000 maps; 100,000 cadastral survey plans and field notes.
Annual accessions: 30 maps.
Area specialization: Province of Ontario.
Subject specializations: ground surveys; historical survey plans; topography; planimetry.
Special cartographic collection: original township plans dating from ca. 1790.
Depository for: Ontario Province.
Serves: government agencies; public.
Interlibrary loan: not available.
Reproduction facility: photocopy.

590 ONTARIO DEPARTMENT OF MINES, LIBRARY. Room 1433, Whitney Block, Parliament Buildings, (2) Tel. 416/365-1352. Lillian A. Burnett, Libn.
Staff: 1 full time; 1 part time.
Size: 9,000 maps; 8 gazetteers.
Annual accessions: 1,000 maps.
Area specialization: Ontario.
Depository for: USGS (geol); Canada.
Serves: public.
Interlibrary loan: not available.
Reproduction facility: Xerox.

591 ONTARIO WATER RESOURCES COMMISSION, DIVISION OF WATER RESOURCES, 40 St. Clair Avenue West, (7) Tel. 416/365-2105. H. A. Flotner, Chief Cartographer.
Staff: 3 part time.
Size: 15,000 maps; 25,000 aerial photographs.

Annual accessions: 1,000 maps.
Area specialization: Ontario.
Subject specializations: water resources; geology; topography.
Depository for: USGS (geol); Canada; Ontario Province.
Serves: public.
Interlibrary loan: not available.
Reproduction facilities: photocopy; Xerox; microfilm; Diazo.

592 UNIVERSITY OF TORONTO, MAP LIBRARY. 100 George Street, (5) Tel. 406/928-3372. Miss Joan Winearls, Map Libn.
Staff: 3 full time; 1 part time.
Size: 61,000 maps; 669 atlases; 1 globe; 7,500 aerial photographs; 125 gazetteers.
Annual accessions: 7,300 maps; 75 atlases; 10 gazetteers.
Area specializations: Ontario; Canada; Europe; South America; Africa.
Subject specialization: geology.
Depository for: USGS (topo, geol); Canada; DOS.
Serves: University; public.
Interlibrary loan: available.
Reproduction facilities: Xerox; microfilm.
Publications: selected acquisitions (bi-monthly); map library brochure.

Waterloo

593 UNIVERSITY OF WATERLOO, DEPARTMENT OF GEOGRAPHY AND PLANNING, MAP LIBRARY. Tel. 519/744-6111, ext. 2795. Edward Sommerville, Map Curator.
Staff: 2 full time; 5 part time.
Size: 20,000 maps; 300 atlases; 50 relief models; 4,000 aerial photographs; 5 gazetteers.
Annual accessions: 2,000 maps; 30 atlases; 500 aerial photographs.
Area specializations: Canada; western Europe.
Depository for: USGS (topo); Canada.
Serves: University; public.
Interlibrary loan: not available.
Reproduction facilities: photocopy; Xerox; Ozalid.
Publication: An Introduction to the Map Library by Edward Sommerville.

QUEBEC

Chicoutimi

594 LA SOCIÉTÉ HISTORIQUE DU SAGUENAY, Postal Box 1005. Tel. 418/549-2805. Victor Tremblay, Archivist.
Staff: 1 part time.
Size: 1,600 maps; 25 atlases; 1 relief model; 50 aerial photographs; 1 gazetteer.
Area specializations: Saguenay; Quebec Province; eastern Canada.
Subject specialization: history.
Serves: public.
Interlibrary loan: not available.
Reproduction facility: Xerox.

Montreal

595 ARCTIC INSTITUTE OF NORTH AMERICA, 3458 Redpath Street, (109) Tel. 514/937-4607. Nora T. Corley, Libn.

Staff: 1 part time.
Size: 10,000 maps; 30 atlases.
Annual accessions: 600 maps.
Area specializations: polar regions; Canadian arctic; Alaskan arctic.
Subject specializations: topography; hydrography.
Depository for: USGS (topo—Alaska); Canada (northern Canada).
Serves: Institute; public.
Interlibrary loan: not available.
Reproduction facility: Xerox.

596 BIBLIOTHÈQUE NATIONALE DU QUÉBEC, DÉPARTEMENT DES DOCUMENTS SPÉCIAUX, 1700 rue Saint-Denis, (129) Tel. 514/873-4488. Mlle. Marguerite Mercier, Directrice.
Size: 3,553 maps; 160 atlases; 1 globe.
Area specializations: Quebec; Canada; North America.
Subject specializations: geology; topography; history.
Special cartographic collections: Atlas Geographique—a collection of 123 old maps; 43 maps by G. Delisle; 26 maps by Johann Homann; 25 maps by Nicolas Visscher. *The American Atlas*—a collection of 76 rare folding maps of North America by Rocque, de la Rochette, Carver, Jefferys, Cook, Lane, Faden, etc; *Amitie Franco-Canadienne*—a collection of maps pertaining to New France.
Depository for: Canada; France (North America only).
Serves: public.
Interlibrary loan: not available.
Reproduction facilities: photocopy; microfilm.

597 ÉCOLE POLYTECHNIQUE, 2500 Marie-Guyard, (250) Tel. 514/739-2451, local 205. Roger Bonin, Libn.
Staff: 1 full time; 1 part time.
Size: 40,000 maps; 10 atlases.
Annual accessions: 3,000 maps.
Subject specializations: topography; geology.
Depository for: Canada; Quebec Province.
Serves: School; public.
Interlibrary loan: not available.

598 McGILL UNIVERSITY, DEPARTMENT OF GEOGRAPHY, UNIVERSITY MAP COLLECTION, (2) Tel. 514/392-5492. C. B. Fay, Map Curator.
Staff: 1 full time; 4 part time.
Size: 60,000 maps; 200 atlases; 10 globes; 50 relief models; 5,000 aerial photographs; 100 gazetteers.
Annual accessions: 5,000 maps; 50 atlases; 500 aerial photographs; 25 gazetteers.
Area specializations: eastern Canada; Arctic; USSR; Latin America; Europe.
Subject specializations: physical, human, and economic geography.
Depository for: USGS (topo, geol); U.S. Census Bureau; Canada (NTS, GSC); USC&GS; DOS; Australia (topo); Guyana Geological Survey.
Serves: University; public.
Interlibrary loan: available.
Reproduction facility: Xerox.

599 McGILL UNIVERSITY, LIBRARY, DEPARTMENT OF RARE BOOKS AND SPECIAL COLLECTIONS, MAP COLLECTION, 3459 McTavish Street, (112) Tel. 514/392-4973. Mrs. G.R. Saunders, Curator.
Staff: 1 part time.
Size: 2,800 maps; 150 atlases; 6 globes.

Annual accessions: 40 maps; 15 atlases.
Area specializations: Canada; North America; West Indies; Caribbean; Europe.
Subject specializations: history; transportation.
Serves: University; public.
Interlibrary loan: not available.
Reproduction facility: Xerox.

600 UNIVERSITÉ DE MONTRÉAL, CARTOTHÈQUE DU DÉPARTMENT DE GÉOGRAPHIE, P.O. Box 6128. Tel. 514/343-7360, Bernard Chouinard, Map Curator.
Staff: 1 full time.
Size: 70,000 maps; 300 atlases; 1 globe; 25 relief models; 6,000 aerial photographs; 40 gazetteers.
Annual accessions: 500 maps; 25 atlases; 600 aerial photographs.
Area specializations: Quebec Province; Canada.
Subject specializations: topography; geology.
Depository for: Canada (NTS, GSC).
Serves: University; public.
Interlibrary loan: not available.

601 UNIVERSITÉ DE MONTRÉAL, DÉPARTMENT OF GEOLOGY, CARTOTHÈQUE, P.B. 6128. Tel. 514/343-6820. Dr. P. P. David, Professor.
Staff: 3-4 part time.
Size: 25,000 maps; 4 atlases; 3 relief models; 3,500 aerial photographs.
Annual accessions: 2,000 maps; 200-400 aerial photographs.
Area specializations: Canada; United States.
Subject specialization: geology.
Depository for: USGS (topo, geol); Canada.
Serves: University; public.
Interlibrary loan: not available.
Reproduction facilities: photocopy; Xerox.

Quebec

602 UNIVERSITÉ LAVAL, BIBLIOTHÈQUE GÉNÉRAL, LA CARTOTHÈQUE, (10e) Tel. 418/656-2002. Yves Tessier, Cartothécaire.
Staff: 1 full time.
Size: 38,257 maps; 752 atlases; 3 globes; 1 relief model; 10,042 aerial photographs; 1 gazetteer.
Annual accessions: 5,500 maps; 100 atlases; 800 aerial photographs.
Area specializations: Quebec; Canada; northeastern United States; France; French Africa; West Indies; Guatemala.
Subject specializations: physical geography; population; land use.
Special cartographic collection: 500 old maps of Quebec and New France.
Depository for: USGS (topo—selective); Canada; Quebec Province; DOS.
Serves: University.
Interlibrary loan: not available.
Reproduction facilities: photocopy; Xerox; microfilm.
Publications: Guide de la Cartothèque. Liste des Principaux Atlas Régionaux de la Cartothèque de l'Université Laval.

SASKATCHEWAN

Regina

603   REGINA PUBLIC LIBRARY, 2311 Twelfth Avenue. Tel. 306/523-7621.
Miss Helen McKay, Head of Adult Services.
Size: 870 maps; 80 atlases; 2 globes; 1 relief model; 20 gazetteers.
Area specialization: Saskatchewan.
Serves: public.
Reproduction facilities: Xerox; microfilm.

604   SASKATCHEWAN ARCHIVES BOARD. A. R. Turner, Provincial
Archivist.
Staff: 1 part time.
Size: 1,370 maps; 13 atlases; 50 aerial photographs.
Annual accessions: 50 maps.
Area specializations: Saskatchewan; Northwest Territories.
Subject specializations: topography; political geography (electoral districts, local
government); railway construction; local history.
Serves: public.
Interlibrary loan: not available.
Reproduction facilities: photocopy; microfilm.

605   UNIVERSITY OF SASKATCHEWAN, DIVISION OF SOCIAL SCIEN-
CES, MAP LIBRARY, Regina campus. Tel. 306/525-0111. A. L.
Bleszynski, Instructor in Geography and Map Libn.
Staff: 3 part time.
Size: 4,000 maps; 35 atlases; 480 aerial photographs.
Annual accessions: 2,500 maps; 25 atlases.
Area specializations: Canada; Great Britain.
Subject specializations: topography; geology; soils; land use; urban planning.
Depository for: Canada.
Serves: University.
Interlibrary loan: not available.

INDEX

The numbers in this index are Entry Numbers, not page numbers.

A

Abajian, James de T., 69
Abelson, Nathaniel O., 375
ACIC (USAF) historical chart
    collection, 310
Adams, Clifford, 192
Adams, R. G., *Clinton Collection (British Headquarters Maps),* 265
Adirondack Mountains, 355
Adirondack Museum, 355
Adolphus (Gustavus) College, 294
Aeromagnetism, 369
Aeronautical charts, 310, 528
Africa, 16, 47, 77, 169, 174, 232, 241, 270, 360, 461, 568, 579, 592
    central, 566
    French, 602
Agee (Rucker) Collection, 2
Agriculture, 186, 313, 362, 461
Air University, 4
Airports, 90
Akron University, 397
Alabama,
    Geological Survey, depository for, 223
    University, Dept. of Geology-Geography, 6
    University, Main Library, 7
Alabama Collection, 7
Alameda County, Calif., 50
Alaska,
    Division of Mines and Geology, 9
    University, 10
Alberta University, 565
Albuquerque Public Library, 344
Alcuin Library, 284
Alderfer, William K., 181
Alderman Library, 516
Alexander, Elizabeth, 135
Alexander, Gerard L., 374
Allan, Helen L., 579
Allen, Virginia, 105
Alward, Emily, 191
Amazon River Valley, 436
American Alpine Club, 366
American Antiquarian Society, 260
The American Atlas, 596

American Automobile Association, 114
American Geographical Society, 367
American Revolutionary War, 126, 129, 265
Ames Library of South Asia, 288
Amherst College, 237
Amitié Franco-Canadienne, 596
Anderson, Martha, 534
Anderson, Norman R., 536
Andre, Leslie, 160
Antarctica, 56, 129, 178, 595
Antioch College, 420
Appalachian Mountains, 213
Archaeology, 11, 221
Architecture, 146
Arctic Institute of North America, 595
Arctic region, 565, 595, 598
Argentina, weather charts, depository for, 290
Arizona,
    Bureau of Mines, 17
    depository for, 13
    Dept. of Library and Archives, 13
    Dept. of Mineral Resources, 14
    State University, 16
    University, 19
Arkansas,
    University, Dept. of Geology, 20
    University, General Library, 21
Armistice lines, 375
Armstrong, Helen J., 171
Ashmore, John D., 4
Asia, 38, 249, 270, 360, 380
    eastern, 27, 90, 169, 294, 363, 419
    southeastern, 151, 169, 171
    southern, 288
Aston, E. H., 39
Atlanta Historical Society, 145
The Atlantic Neptune, 226, 584
Atlas Geographique, 596
Atmospheric Sciences Library, 236
Auburn University, 1
Augustana College, 179
Aull, Sara, 502
Australasia, 151
Australia, 178, 180, 563, 572
    depository for, 51, 367, 572, 598
Automated Nautical Chart Information File (ANCIF), 131
Aviation Cartography, 129

139

School of Mines, 95
State Historical Society, 91
State University, 94
University, 86
Colorado Plateau, 11
Colpitts, Corinne D., 425
Colson, Judith, 575
Columbia University, 368
Columbus Memorial Library, 120
Comer, Ann, 234
Commerce, 289
Communications, 124
Computer printed book catalog of
    the map collection, Univ. of
    Calif., Santa Cruz, 78
Comstock mining area, 323
Confederate Museum Library, 520
Connecticut Historical Society, 100
Connecticut State Library, 101
Connecticut University, 109
Connette, Earle, 528
Conservation, 278
Contra Costa County Library, 53
Cook County, Ill., 162
Cooley, Marguerite B., 13
Cooper, Myrtle, 312
Cordts, Gertrude M., 50
Corley, Nora T., 595
Cornell, Greta, 376
Cornell University,
    Center for Aerial Photographic
        Studies, 362
    Olin (John M.) Library, 363
Cossitt-Goodwyn Libraries, 481
Costa Rica-Panama, boundary, 85
County maps and atlases, 182, 206,
    227, 231, 247, 374
Covalt, Jean T., 52
Cowan (Robert E.) collection of
    California and the Pacific
    West, 46
Cramer, Robert E., 390
Crane, William H., 190
Crawford County, Pa., 449
Crawford County Historical Society,
    449
Cross (Wilbur) Library, 109
Crown Collection of American Maps,
    16, 45
Cultural geography, 28, 535
Culver, Jerry B., 546
Cumming, John, 282
Cumming, William P., 391
Curran, Terence, 570
Current Geographical Publications,
    367
Curtis, Gordon, 72
Cushing, John D., 245
Cutler, Kathryn N., 82

D

Dafoe (Elizabeth) Library, 574
Dalhousie University, 576
Dallas Public Library, 491
Dallman, Carol, 300
Dando, William A., 232
Darlington Memorial Library, 457
Dartmouth College, 326
David, P. P., 601
Davies, Mrs. Robert, 497
Davis, Dorothy Gae, 271
Davis, Michael E., 198
Day, Dorothy, 466
Day, James M., 486
Dayton and Montgomery County
    Public Library, 412
Degitz, Dalton, 64
DeGolyer Collection, 493
Delaware Historical Society, 112
Delaware State Archives, 110
Delaware University, 111
Demography, 334, 451, 461, 510,
    602
DeMott, Lawrence L., 175
Denison University, 413
Dennis, Margaret, 436
Denoyer-Geppert Company, 166
Denver Public Library, 89
Denver Research Center Library, 97
Denver University, 93
Depauw University, 191
Des Barres, J. F. W., *The Atlantic
    Neptune,* 226, 584
*A Descriptive List of Treasure Maps
    and Charts,* 129
De Smet (Father) Collection, 528
Deter, Francis H., Jr., 118
Detroit and Vicinity before 1900,
    129
Detroit Public Library,
    Burton Historical Collection, 266
    History and Travel Dept., 267
Detroit Regional Transportation and
    Land Use Study, 268
deValinger, Jeon, Jr., 110
Devere, Joseph, 53
De Vries, Mary K., 263
De Vries Collection, 29
Diamond Shamrock Chemical
    Company, 406
Dienes, Mrs. Jennie, 210
Discovery and exploration, 2, 89,
    103, 167, 185, 265, 289, 318,
    370, 426, 469, 537
District of Columbia Public Library,
    Central Library, History,
    Geography, and Government
    Division, 121

Central Library, Washingtoniana
Division, 122
Georgetown Branch, 123
Doherty, Marianne, 164
Donkin, Kate, 578
Donnell, Marianne, 140
Dorsey, James, 60
Douglas Library, 580
Douglass, Dorris, 145
Dowd, Sheila, 28
Drazniowsky, Roman, 367
Drouillard, Beverly L., 586
Duer, Margaret D., 142
Duke University, 389
Dunkle, William M., 259
Dunlap, Ann B., 486
Dunn, Caroline, 193
Duprey, Wilson G., 373
Durrance, Raymond E., 530

E

Eagon, Carrie W., 498
Earth sciences, 171, 368
East Carolina University, 390
East Orange Public Library, 331
East Tennessee State University, 478
Eastern Illinois University, 160
Eastern Michigan University, 283
Eastern New Mexico University, 348
Eastern Washington State College,
525
Eastern Washington State Historical
Society, 533
Easton, William W., 178
Ebersole, William Dale, Jr., 419
École Polytechnique, 597
Economic geography, 171, 261, 319,
409, 445, 524, 579, 585, 598
Edwards, G. P., 426
Eggleston Library, 517
Eisen, Marc M., 331
Ejlali, Majid, 478
Enders, Gertrude, 132
Engineering, 362
Engineering Societies Library, 369
Erhardt, Davis, 365
Erie County, N. Y., 358
Essex County, Mass., 255
Essex Institute, 255
ESSO Production Research Library,
498
Europe, 167, 248-9, 294, 360, 380,
385, 399, 440, 574, 592,
598-9
central, 68, 186, 461
collection of pre-World War II
maps, 169
eastern, 487
western, 126, 186, 230, 461, 493,
593

Eutsler, Luella S., 417
Explorers Club, 370
Explorers' routes, 129, 475

F

Facsimiles of Rare Historical Maps,
129
Faden (William) collection of French
and Indian and Revolutionary
War maps, 129
Fairleigh Dickinson University, 340
Farnsworth, Roy L., 224
Fay, C. B., 598
*Federal Exploration of the American
West Before 1880,* 130
Fentress, Roy, 370
Ferguson map of Tucson, 1862, 18
Ferries, 147
Fessenden, Robert E., 433
Fillmore (Millard) collection of 19th
century maps, 129
Fleming, Helen, 293
Fleming, Janice, 473
Flint Community Junior College, 271
The Flint Journal, 272
Florida,
Board of Conservation, 139
State University, 140
University, University Library,
136
University, Yonge Library of
Florida History, 135
Florida Atlantic University, 133
Flood control, 300, 479
Flotner, H. A., 591
Fogarty, Catherine M., 340
Fogle, Elizabeth, 400
Fogler (Raymond H.) Library, 225
Fondren Library, 500
Force, Ronald W., 410
Fort Wayne and Allen County Public
Library, 190
Fort Worth Public Library, 496
Fortney, Mary E., 174
Forts, 147
Foscue (Edwin J.) Map Library, 493
Fountain Valley School, 87
Fox, Alan, 246
Framptom (Jerome) Library, 234
France, 602
depository for, 180, 259, 596
Frazer, Georgia A., 500
Freeman, Ellen L., 189
French and Indian War maps, 129
Fresno State College, 35
Friedenson, Mrs. Daniel, 241
Frollicher, Ruth, 315
Frontier history, 318
Frostburg State College, 234
Fulton County, Ga., 145

New York Public Library,
Bulletin, 374
Map Division, 374
New Zealand, 572
Newark Public Library, 336
Newberry Library, 167
Newman (Carol M.) Library, 514
Newport Historical Society, 464
Newsome, Jeanette, 7
Newton, Milton B., 219
Niagara Peninsula, 578
Nicoletti, Frank T., 124
Nikola, Charles E., 383
North America, 86, 89, 200, 249,
313
coasts, 530
eastern, 126
manuscript maps, 168
western, 25, 34
North Carolina,
Dept. of Archives and History,
391
State University, 392
University, Geology Dept., 387
University, Library, 388
North Carolina in Maps, 391
North Dakota,
State University, 393
University, Geography Dept., 394
University, Geology Library, 395
North Texas State University, 494
Northeastern Boundary Commission
official atlas, 1815-1840, 226
Northern Arizona Museum, 11
Northern Arizona University, 12
Northern College of Applied Arts and
Technology, 577
Northern Illinois University, 171
Northern Michigan University, 280
Northwest Territories, Canada, 604
Northwestern University,
Grant Memorial Library of
Geology, 173
Map Library, 174
Norwich University, 512
Notre Dame University
Geology Library, 196
Memorial Labrary, 197
Nowaki, Junko Ida, 150

O

Oakland Public Library, 50
Oceanography, 56, 169, 173, 178,
259, 338, 530
Oceans, 40, 131, 259
Odell, Clarence B., 166
Official Maps–War of the Rebellion,
5
Ohio,
city directories, 414

counties, 411
Historical Society, 408
southwestern, 401
State Library, 411
State University, Map Library,
409
State University, Orton Memorial
Library of Geology, 410
University, 398
Ohio River Valley, 193
Oil and gas, 39, 74, 97, 189, 425,
490, 492-3, 496, 563
Oklahoma,
counties, 422
County Libraries, 423
Dept. of Libraries, 424
State University, 425
University, 422
Old Northwest Territory, 185, 193,
278, 282, 407
Olin (John M.) Library, 363
Olson, John K., 313
Olson Library, 280
Omaha Public Library, 320
Oneida County, N. Y. 382
Ontario,
depository for, 589, 591
eastern, 579
Lands and Forests Dept., 589
Mines Dept., 590
Mines Dept., depository for, 577
southern, 578
townships, 589
Water Resources Commission,
591
Orange County, Calif.,
aerial photographs, 55
State College, 36
Oregon,
Historical Society, 433
State Highway Dept., depository
for, 433
State Library, 435
State University, 430
University, 431
Oriental collection of rare
manuscript and printed maps
and atlases, 129
Orton Library Notes, 410
Orton Memorial Library of Geology,
410
Ossining, N. Y., 376
Ossining Historical Society Museum,
376
Ottawa University, 586
Ozanne collection of manuscript
views and maps of the
Revolutionary War, 129

151

Scandinavia, 179
Scannell, Karen, 70
Schell, Mary, 61
Schiffner, Judith A., 304
Schimmelpfeng, R. H., 109
Schneider, Mrs. G. K., 380
Scholberg, Henry, 288
Schonfeld, Josef, 567
School districts, 206
Schoolfield, Dudley B., 492
Schoyer, George, 409
Schulz, Herbert C., 75
Scripps Institution of Oceanography, 40
Scriven, Margaret, 161
Seaberg, Lillian, 136
Seaborn, Mrs. Davis, 476
Seamster, Florance P., 517
Seattle Public Library, 529
Seelye, Mary, 154
Selected List of Maps and Charts (Tennessee Valley Authority), 479
Selected Maps and Charts of Antarctica, 129
Sermon, Mrs. S., 316
Settlement, 426
Shearman (Warren C.) collection of 17th and 18th century map makers, 46
Sheffield, Dennis M., 119
Sheridan College, 562
Sherman (William T.) Collection of Civil War maps, 129
Shields, Mai N., 54
Shipton, Nathaniel N., 265
Shirk, Frank C., 514
Shivers, Sue, 122
Shrewsbury, Mary E., 9
Shultz, Irvil P., 92
Sierecki, Joan, 162
Sierra Club, 72
Sierra Nevada, 72
Simms, Eric, 22
Simon Fraser University, 566
Sivers, Robert, 77
Slippery Rock State College, 459
Slothower, Margaret, 180
Small, Louise, 318
Smith, Betsey, 443
Smith, Clifton, 76
Smith, Harriet W., 184
Smith, Hope S., 56
Smith, Marcia, 355
Smith, Winifred, 148
Smith (Sanderson) Collection, 380
Smith College, 254
Smith (John) map of Virginia, 1612, 129
Smith (William S.) Library, 148
Smythe, Olive M., 222

Social sciences, 288
Society for the Preservation of New England Antiquities, 247
Society of California Pioneers, 73
Soil Research Institute, 585
Soils, 34, 55, 128, 164, 263, 421, 455, 477, 493, 549, 579, 585, 605
Sommerville, Edward, 593
South America, 28, 90, 221, 313, 367, 371, 440, 592
South Carolina,
    Archives and History Dept., 469
    University, McKissick Memorial Library, 470
    University, South Caroliniana Library, 471
South Caroliniana Library, 471
South Dakota,
    boundaries, 475
    School of Mines and Technology, 474
    State Historical Society, 473
    University, 475
South Florida University, 141
South Georgia College, 148
Southard, Eugenia M., 227
Southeastern Wisconsin Regional Planning Commission, 555
Southern Illinois University,
    Lovejoy Library, 172
    Science Library, 159
Southern Methodist University, 493
Southwest Room, Albuquerque Public Library, 344
Spain, 178, 371
Spellman, Lawrence E., 339
Spokane Public Library, 534
Sprague, Theodore S., 414
Sprankle, Anita T., 446
Spreng, A. C., 305
Sprenger, Bernice C., 266
Squier (Ephraim G.) Collection of maps of Central America, 129
Standard Oil Company of California, 74
Stanford University,
    Library, 81
    School of Earth Sciences, 82
Stanislas State College Library, 83
Stark County, Ohio, 400
Starkey, Virginia, 91
Starr, Dorothy, 267
Staten Island Institute of Arts and Sciences, 380
Stephens, J. Kent, 32
Stephenson, Andrew D., 57
Stephenson, Robert E., 514
Stevens, Stanley D., 78
Stewart, George, 2
Stewart Collection of Jerseyana, 332

155